MINDFULNESS
MEDITATIONS
for STRESS

MINDFULNESS MEDITATIONS

for STRESS

100 Simple Practices to Ease Tension and Find Peace

Denise G. Dempsey, MEd

**ROCKRIDGE
PRESS**

For general information on our other products and services or to obtain technical support, please contact our Customer Care Department within the United States at (866) 744-2665, or outside the United States at (510) 253-0500.

Rockridge Press publishes its books in a variety of electronic and print formats. Some content that appears in print may not be available in electronic books, and vice versa.

Interior and Cover Designer: Carlos Esparza
Art Producer: Janice Ackerman
Editor: Erin Nelson
Production Manager: Michael Kay
Production Editor: Sigi Nacson

Cover Photography: © 2020 Madhav Misha/shutterstock and kubais/shutterstock

ISBN: Print 978-1-64739-901-6 | Ebook 978-1-64739-902-3

R0

*To the many meditation teachers who have
helped so many seeking peace.
To the scientists taking knowledge of
meditation to a new level.
Much gratitude.*

CONTENTS

A NOTE FROM
THE EDITOR

Dear Reader,

I first met Denise Dempsey via video chat when she was sitting outside of a bungalow in Hawaii, where she had traveled to teach a meditation workshop. The sky glimmered and the palm trees swayed, but Denise wasn't interested in paradise. Centered and present, she wanted to get to business, distilling her knowledge around mindfulness into 100 meditations that could help people manage the stress, both large and small, impeding their life.

Do a quick internet search and you will find thousands of resources on mindfulness, meditation, and the secrets to being present. Many of them are helpful; few are transformative. What makes Denise stand out is her refusal to offer quick fixes and lofty promises. Her commitment is to the hard work of mindfulness. Her duty is to the reader, whom she is able to meet exactly where they are. The result is a thoughtful and accessible path to meditation by someone who has known fear and heartbreak, who has overcome hardship and transformed it into a gift to guide others.

There are many ways to incorporate mindfulness practices into your life. What's certain is that no matter what stage you are on in your journey, no matter what type of stress brought you here, Denise will meet you with compassion, diligence, and support. I hope you get the same comfort and inspiration from her words as I do.

One breath at a time,

Erin C. Nelson
Editor, Callisto Media

INTRODUCTION

This book exists at a time when meditation is no longer a fringe practice. Scientific research has paved the way for its entry into healthcare, in a way measuring wisdom that's been there all along. We now have access to a multitude of resources—meditation apps, guided meditation recordings, and books. Yet amid this need for support, many also desire greater simplicity where one does not have to rely on apps or recordings. It's in this context that I offer a different kind of meditation book.

What you have here is a special selection of meditations that can be used to help you manage stress. Whether your stress is high or low, acute or chronic, this book offers ways to peacefully tend to your needs. Regardless of the time of day, whether you have a surplus or lack of time, you'll find meditations here that address a variety of needs. As you'll discover, mindfulness practice becomes more familiar as you go. When there are challenges, there are also ways to address those challenges.

In my thirties, I was introduced to mindfulness meditation in a way that was simple and practical. This was through the Mindfulness-Based Stress Reduction (MBSR) program, founded in 1979 by the "father of mindfulness" in the mainstream, Jon Kabat-Zinn. The MBSR program and mindfulness became a core component of behavioral medicine when researchers began to rely on them to study how contemplative practice could benefit mind-body health. Through experience, I have learned that the practice doesn't need to be complicated, difficult, or time-consuming.

Meditation has brought ease into my life—a growing acceptance of myself, my moods, and my body. It has helped me manage several health issues, including the diagnosis of a brain tumor, which, I was told, would probably not kill me but I would have to learn to live with it nonetheless. Mindfulness meditation ultimately quieted the noise of that stress. My performance at work also improved. There seemed to be more time, even though nothing had tangibly changed. Using other methods, I had been meditating since my teens, but this was a new beginning.

Since becoming an MBSR teacher in 2003, I've taught thousands of students while working within multiple healthcare systems and for the US Department of Veteran Affairs. People sign up for the classes I teach because they're experiencing symptoms that all relate, in some way, to "stress." These students want to feel better. They often report later that, like me, they found that the skills they developed remained useful long after they addressed the initial problem. "A journey of a thousand miles begins with a single step," the ancient philosopher Lao Tzu said. This book is here to support you on your path.

HOW TO USE THIS BOOK

When we experience chronic stress, sometimes even our best go-to strategies don't seem to help anymore, and we benefit from new ones. The 100 mindfulness meditations you have in this book cover everything from everyday stress—like dealing with traffic or situations at work—to the stress of chronic health conditions. These meditations can help you take care of your body when you're feeling stressed. They can also increase your resilience to stress so that it takes less of a toll.

This is a book you can carry around with you or keep by your bedside. Here's a big tip about books that has benefited me: Don't try to keep it in mint condition. Dog-ear your favorite pages. Let the cover become worn from carrying it around with you. The best books ultimately become worn and tattered, a sign of being well loved. You may also appreciate keeping a journal to reflect on your experiences or to make notes.

This book is written to be useful. It is something you can turn to when you are stressed or overwhelmed. A variety of meditations are offered, and they are presented in the simplest way so that the words don't overwhelm. You won't need to rely on apps or recordings. You can always come back to the book, but you may also find that the practices are simple, flexible, and ultimately portable because you can make them your own.

There are three parts to this book, and you can turn to any section any-time. There's no need to start at the beginning; it's fine to jump around. Part I offers background information on mindfulness, meditation, and stress, and is accompanied by foundational meditations. Part II focuses on meditations to target specific stress responses or stressful situations. Any and all of these can be a support, depending on your needs. Part III supports your ongoing practice with accessible movement meditations and five-minute meditations that are easy to access as you continue through your life. All the meditations here are described in simple enough form that you won't have to keep looking at the book. You can just practice with what you remember.

This book is not just for beginners. For experienced meditators, this book can provide support and inspiration as well as ideas for how to prac-tice forms of meditation that may be less familiar. I hope this book can be like a friend and a resource that helps you keep your practice fresh.

Whereas apps and guided recordings can be great supports, the sim-plicity of self-guided practice is often easier to access. This book can also be a complement to the many other rich and wonderful books (see the Resources section at the back of the book) or meditation classes available in your community.

When we're stressed or overwhelmed, we benefit from simplicity. I intend for these 100 meditations to be easy and comforting to read when you're stressed or overwhelmed. I hope you enjoy the meditations here for a long time to come. They can grow with you as you develop your mindfulness and stress-reduction skills. Wishing you many moments of mindfulness, supportive meditation, and a relaxed life!

PART I

Foundational Meditations

In these beginning chapters, we'll cover the connection between mindfulness, meditation, and stress. You'll see answers to common questions that arise for all levels of mindfulness practitioners and get a better sense of how it all works. Foundational information is followed by 20 basic meditations for the mind and body, based on traditional breathing and awareness practices that have guided humans for millennia.

On using a timer: Some meditations will ask you to use a timer so that, in the face of any restlessness or desire to quit, you have provided yourself with a kind of container for practice. Other meditations are less formal and oriented toward any amount of time you can offer yourself.

Mindfulness, Meditation, and Stress

Our bodies are designed to be resilient. Mindfulness and meditation can increase our ability to adapt to stress, reducing its negative effects. The benefits are not in our imagination. Knowing a little bit more about these benefits can remove some of the mystery around mindfulness and meditation, and open us up to learning a new practice.

What Is Mindfulness?

The word "mindfulness" means simply to pay attention or be aware. The practice of it, however, is more a way of being, supported by a specific mindset and attitude. In the moment, we have access to the choices that can lead our bodies and minds back into balance. When stress is taking its toll on our body, the addition of mindfulness can be transformative. As we tend to say in my programs, it's not the stress, but how we handle it that can make all the difference.

I have heard of people recounting a fear that mindfulness could make them lose their edge, cause them to become passively tolerant or even like an emotionless zombie! On the contrary, mindfulness is sometimes referred to as a kind of wise attention. It isn't a fixed state of mind but one that is flexible and can reflect our needs and priorities in the moment. In any given moment, there are countless things that can draw our attention. Mindfulness can be like an added clarity.

Whether responding to stress or enjoying life's pleasures, meeting each moment with mindfulness is a way of reclaiming a life lost to distractedness. And it's not just one way of paying attention. We can vary *how* we pay attention. At times we may want to tighten or narrow our focus, like the light of a laser pointer. Or we could take a broader view, like a spotlight or search beam.

Mindfulness becomes a tool to help with stress when we link it with certain attitudes. These reflect values like kindness, patience, curiosity, and an open mind. As an example, the absence of kindness can make mindfulness more like a state of stoic resolve. Without curiosity, we can get stuck in assumptions of how things will turn out. Impatience usually just leads to more tension. If we merely brace ourselves to endure stress, we can lose touch with the fact that we can handle it and maybe even enjoy life more in spite of feeling stressed.

When we start to explore the practice of mindfulness, we may find that it's not as easy as it sounds. For this reason, developing our mindfulness skills through meditation helps us hone certain qualities that naturally carry over into our daily life. When we practice routinely, it takes less and less effort to draw upon these skills. The more perspective we have on stress, the less rigid our attitude and the more choices available for responding to it in a healthy way.

What Is Meditation?

Meditation offers ways of cultivating mind-body awareness and useful perspectives that also help us know ourselves better, manage stress, and support our bodies to be more resilient. Even though it has spiritual origins, as a modern practice it is used by many people around the world to develop emotional and physical resilience and an overall sense of well-being.

Although we may come to meditation hoping to immediately feel peace of mind or ease in the body, it is common not to feel the benefits *while* meditating, especially during shorter meditations. We are more likely to feel the positive effects later in the day—or even the next day. We learn to practice for its own sake, so the benefits can accumulate and we can feel happier and more resilient, no matter what life throws our way.

These are the basic forms of meditation:

concentration (also referred to as serenity practice)

open monitoring (just sitting with awareness)

insight practice (where we mindfully investigate our inner experience)

mantra meditation (repetition of a sound, a word, or a phrase)

loving-kindness meditation (cultivating the spirit of goodwill for others and ourselves)

mindful self-compassion (soothing or comforting ourselves)

Researchers are studying each of these forms of meditation to learn more about how the mind works, and how we can use them to improve our health and well-being. They are all equally valuable forms of meditation.

Stress Level

| Low | Moderate | High |

What Do We Mean by "Stress"?

Resilience and stress both exist on a spectrum. Regardless of how stressful our lives are, when we are resilient, we return to the part of the spectrum where stress is low and manageable. This is a healthy body and mind. Chronic stress, however, shows up like wear and tear. We may experience things like fatigue, irritability, and an increase in chronic pain levels as our immunity decreases. Chronic health issues might get worse when we're under stress.

So, what's happening in the body when we are stressed? The stress reaction starts with perception. You likely won't notice when the brain signals the body to send a messenger, the stress hormone cortisol, to mobilize a system response called a "stress reaction." During this stress reaction, we first become more alert. Our heart rate and blood pressure may increase, and there's an increase in blood flow to the arms and legs. Meanwhile, our digestion temporarily becomes less of a priority. The stress reaction is a natural aspect of our resilience network, which includes our immune system, the balance of blood sugar in our system, and the brain hormones that control our mood.

The good news is that there are ways to address stress so that it takes less of a toll on both mind and body. Mindfulness is a method proven to help. It has now been studied by scientists for over 40 years using state-of-the-art programs like Mindfulness-Based Stress Reduction (MBSR). This book will provide a way to draw on mindfulness techniques so that you can easily help yourself manage stress and thrive.

How Mindfulness Eases Stress

On the spectrum of stress, in even just a single moment, mindfulness can help us regain perspective. At any point in the cascading stress reaction, we may better recognize healthy options for taking care of ourselves or notice our attitude and potentially shift it in a helpful direction. We might ask ourselves if we are making assumptions about how things will turn out or question our worries. We may notice our limiting self-beliefs and remember our capabilities. On the level of emotions, we can invite self-compassion when we are suffering, and we can reach out to get help.

One of the most stressful human experiences is a sense of having no control. A mindful response to stress can help us return to balance more quickly and influence the way this process unfolds. In this way, mindfulness gives us more control. Mindfulness isn't passive at all.

By becoming aware of the ways in which we do have control, we can minimize the stress response. Under circumstances when we have no control, we can support ourselves to self-care in a healthy way that encourages and even builds our resilience. In this way, a mindful approach to life can help us find balance, no matter what is going on.

How Do I Know If It's Stress?

Through the practice of mindfulness, we get better at reading our body signals that relate to stress. For example, physical discomfort may mean that we need to rest, or it could mean we need to move more or honor some emotional needs. Fatigue, restlessness, or agitation could relate to our state of mind or body. The long and short of it is that mindfulness can help us question assumptions and investigate what's happening, not just what we *think* is happening. We can then explore a range of options available to take care of ourselves, including using the meditations in this book. When in doubt, check with your healthcare provider. Stress symptoms may also reflect symptoms of certain health issues.

Cognitive Behavioral Techniques

Although we may come to meditation because we'd like to experience a calmer mind or body, it's quite common to notice things we'd rather not feel while we are doing it. Like most meditators, sometimes when I sit down to meditate, I may become aware of feelings that I did not realize were there. Unpleasant emotions often top the list of things people would rather avoid. We also may prefer not to notice things like restlessness, boredom, agitation, and fatigue. The thing is, we don't have to get rid of thoughts and feelings in order to have a greater sense of inner balance and perspective. It's a matter of learning to relate or respond to them differently.

This leads many to ask, Why would anyone want to feel uncomfortable during meditation? The answer is that the practice is not only for "right now" but to help us cultivate qualities that serve us in the long run, including when things happen that are out of our control. If we habitually detach, we may lose touch with the richness of life, as well as opportunities to respond consciously and creatively. Many meditators, myself included, have found that life and relationships go more smoothly when our meditation skills transfer over to daily life. What's more, we often take better care of ourselves when our inner life becomes known to us.

In this section, you'll find some cognitive behavioral skills, the things we can do in response to mental habits and tendencies that otherwise may lead to greater tension or frustration. These are often taught during mindfulness meditation training in MBSR classes.

MAKE SPACE

Create room for feelings, without adding anything further to the story. Emotions are not permanent conditions. Consider emotions as though they were a river or stream. Sometimes it's as though we fall in and get carried downstream. When we become aware that we're in the stream, we can climb back out onto the bank and watch it flow by.

Observe thoughts or emotions as you might watch clouds coming and going across the sky. Notice how these, as well as sensations, are ever-changing. Whatever is happening, take the attitude of a relatively neutral observer. Get curious about what is happening and let go of assumptions about how things are going to turn out. You can picture thoughts as though projected on a movie screen. In the audience, you also know that what's happening on the screen is not actually occurring. Keep in mind that life does not tend to follow the scripts we create in our minds.

PAIN AS SENSATION

Meditation includes the body. When your experience of the body gets your attention, you can try to view discomfort as a constellation of physical sensations. For example, tension may involve many different sensations: pressure, tingling, burning, vibrating, firmness, softness, and so on. If there's something unpleasant that continues to arise in awareness, recognize that it can slip out of awareness, too. Be willing to drop a thought or move attention to something neutral. Mindfulness here is a response; it is not a passive experience or a state of stoic resolve.

You may also notice that physical tension can reflect various emotions. Be gentle with yourself. Don't raise the bar too high. There's no need to feel overly challenged in order to grow with meditation. Self-compassion can be a great response to an inner critic or during times when it's hard to be vulnerable. To gain perspective during meditation, rather than analyzing, simply note qualities—"liking" or "not liking," "pleasant" or "unpleasant," even "neutral." See if you can observe the ways they are constantly changing.

A Word on Extreme Stress

The meditations in this book can be a great support during periods of stress, but at times greater support is necessary. If your levels of stress are extreme, please consider the support of a therapist or talk to your doctor. Extreme stress could cause you to feel unable to cope in a healthy way. It's normal for emotions to fluctuate, even rise in intensity, but if they feel unmanageable, reach out for help. Self-destructive behavior can also be a manifestation of extreme stress.

It's not healthy or wise to use mindfulness or meditation to endure physical difficulties that require medical support. When in doubt, reach out. Remember, there are helping professionals available for support if you feel particularly overwhelmed. It could be wise to talk with someone for some added support and understanding. Furthermore, there are classes and teachers where you can get additional support for exploring meditation. (See Resources, page 174, for more on that.)

The Attitudes of Mindfulness

Mindfulness is based on certain attitudes as much as it is a specific way of paying attention. They are curiosity, patience, non-striving, letting go, acceptance, loving-kindness and self-trust, nonjudgment, and beginner's mind. Here are some examples of how you might draw upon them.

Restlessness (mind or body): Invite patience, let go of assumptions. Get curious about what's happening. Notice what's on your mind. Let it be.

Sleepiness: The only problem with sleepiness is when we think it's a problem. Accepting it and engaging curiosity could activate some additional alertness.

Boredom: Be curious about your experience of the present, on the level of sensations, mental activity, and emotions. Recognize how things are constantly changing. Let go of assumptions that you know what will happen next. Let go of striving. The possibilities are endless.

Doubt: We are cultivating self-trust. Remind yourself that a reason we practice is so we can be resilient during all types of conditions, not just the ones we enjoy or consider most interesting. Remind yourself that you cannot feel all the beneficial changes happening in mind or body while you're meditating.

Rumination: When you become aware of thinking, consider that whatever is on your mind is related to the experience of thinking. Note "thinking" and return to the focus you have chosen for the meditation. Let go of assumptions that you know for sure how things will go. Get curious about what is happening, physically and emotionally.

Discomfort (emotional or physical): Invite self-compassion if you're suffering. Just for now, let go of trying to fix it or change anything. Let go of the assumption that you know how things will turn out. If you feel like stopping, practice the "six-second rule": Make a deal with yourself that you will continue to meditate for a full six seconds, and then reevaluate.

Self-criticism: Practice loving-kindness, self-compassion, and non-striving; remind yourself that you're doing the best you can. Be gentle with your expectations. Notice that self-criticism is just a thought.

Practicing Meditation

Rather than monitor each meditation session for immediate results, it's helpful to do it for its own sake, even when it feels like nothing is happening. This is known as a meditation "practice." Like working out or playing an instrument, if we do it routinely, the benefits add up. Just like doing push-ups can make our arms stronger, meditation can strengthen our coping strategies and improve our resilience to stress.

Each meditation in this book contains guidance for how to meditate in specific ways, but this section offers more on how to generally set yourself up for success.

We tend to have a nonstop flow of things we want to or must do. Meditation is unique, because although it's something we *do*, it can look or feel like not a lot is happening. As you turn your intention toward meditation time, I recommend you think of just the first step, which is like changing gears. It's as much a mental shift as it is something physical. Once you have turned your attention toward meditation, the next step is to find your meditation spot.

Your Meditation Spot

The place where you meditate doesn't have to be perfect. The meditations in this book will give suggestions for where to meditate, but any number of spots might work well. It could be a relatively quiet room, or a place you can be undisturbed. Some people have made a car their meditation spot, because it is the only location where they have privacy. A bathroom stall can be a great meditation spot, and you can also meditate in places like a backyard, a back deck, a park, or someplace at work where you have some privacy.

The more effort required to make the transition, the more likely it will not happen. Convenience is helpful. If you're out in public and you have some time to meditate, just sit with your eyes softly focused, gazing downward. Or hold your phone to your ear as though listening. I did this once, while standing in a park. The funny thing was that another person talking on their phone came and stood nearby.

Position or Posture

The best position for meditation is the one that provides enough comfort to relax, but in an alert way. You may find that circumstances or a physical condition influence the position you choose. Some people have an idea that "real" meditators sit on the floor, on a cushion. That might be true in a monastery, but don't feel limited by props or ideals. Here are just a few ways to position yourself for a meditation.

Lying down: You can meditate lying down on the floor, a bed, the couch, a lounge chair, a lawn chair, in a bathtub. Anyplace that allows for a relative amount of comfort and alertness can work.

Sitting: You can sit in a relatively comfortable chair, on the couch, in a dentist's chair, in a waiting room, on a plane, on a porch swing. You can sit on the floor or on a cushion or on your knees. Get the idea? The main thing is that your posture is intentional and will generally support a relaxed alertness.

What to do with your hands: Typically, during meditation, hands rest gently in your lap or alongside your body.

Standing: If you've chosen standing as your posture, keep your eyes open to assist with balance. Sometimes people choose to stand to increase alertness or support other needs, such as to alleviate chronic pain that is activated in other positions.

Eyes open or closed: Some meditation traditions involve meditating with eyes open. Mindfulness meditation generally suggests closing the eyes. This is predominantly to limit distraction. If you meditate with eyes open, choose a single spot to gently focus your gaze. You may notice that when the mind has wandered, you'll also become aware that the eyes have moved away from the spot.

Movement: During a walking meditation, meditators typically walk quietly back and forth in a space of about 10 to 15 paces. There are other mindful movement meditations that can be useful, especially when feeling agitated. There are also body awareness practices like yoga, tai chi, and qigong that can be great ways to meditate while involving some motion.

Minding the Mind

Here is a list of ways to honor the mind while you practice mindfulness.

Accept that the mind will wander. When you accept that your mind will wander, you free yourself from a restriction that has held back many meditators.

Remember that thoughts are not a problem. In fact, far from it! Awareness is a central element of mindfulness. To notice thoughts is like having an inside view of your working mind, an important reflection of brain health. Each time you notice that you've become lost in thought, you're harnessing the power of awareness. This puts you in position for a conscious response.

Consider creating categories of thoughts. An option for responding to thoughts rather than simply "noting" them is to be aware of the various categories they may fall under. Most of the time we are not aware that we are thinking. In fact, our thoughts are just one aspect of our perception—one angle, one circumstance, a glimmer of perception, an opinion, worry, memory, plan—the list goes on.

Embrace randomness. The mind likes to be stimulated. If there isn't anything to think about, it will randomly find things for you to consider!

Release efforts to control the mind. Imagine someone suddenly walked by with a hot apple pie, fresh from the oven. It would be hard to tune it out. We don't decide to notice the scent of the pie any more than we decide that we're hungry. The same goes for emerging noises. If a sound arises, depending on how strong your concentration, it will get your attention. If it's loud enough, you may even flinch. Cognition is not the only avenue of perception.

Remain curious. Our brain takes care of perception that often tells us how to react. Becoming curious about what's on your mind instead of trying to control thoughts, emotions, or impulses puts you in a better position to choose a conscious response. Things like our plans, memories, or worries are just one element of brain activity. For instance, say you want to pick up something heavy, but when you do, it's lighter than you realized. You may lose your balance or stumble for a moment. The cerebellum, a part of the brain at the back of the head, has done its best to estimate how heavy the object is and how much effort to exert. You may have had the experience of slamming on your brakes before you even formally became aware of a dangerous traffic situation. Several areas of your brain noticed and reacted before it got to the part we tend to relate to as "thinking."

Recognize "reacting" versus "responding." An impulse to react to thoughts, feelings, or sensations often arises automatically. The practice here is to notice and observe thoughts without reacting to them. If there are reactions (emotions or impulses, for instance), mindful responses can be drawn upon.

Minding the Body

Mindfulness includes the body. The aim is to embody the body, experiencing it as it is. Try to distinguish between mental states or thoughts about the body and your direct experience of being alive.

Thoughts about the body might involve memories, judgments, ideas, knowledge, opinions, concerns, plans, and worries. Direct sensory experience, on the other hand, consists of things like pressure, tingling, buzzing, itching, dampness, dryness, warmth, coolness, softness, firmness, sharp sensations, dull sensations, lightness, or heaviness. There might also be sleepiness, restlessness, agitation, boredom, or others. There may be a sense of stillness.

The sensory clarity we can experience through the body is a foundation of mindfulness practice. The following factors are also involved in meditation practice.

TIME OF DAY

Identify a few times during the day when you could conveniently go to one of your meditation spots that you have identified in advance. Often the first part of the day and the last part of the day are more predictable. Clues for best times to practice may come from recognizing your existing routines and connecting meditation to one of them. For example, after arriving home from errands or work, just sit on the couch or drop into a comfortable chair and meditate. Your best time might be after finishing a meal or getting home from walking the dog.

OTHER PEOPLE

When it's helpful, let those who might be affected know that this is something you are doing for better health. When it comes to pets and children, sometimes it's easiest to let them come and go rather than trying to completely get away. The support or tolerance of others can be a great help, even if meditation is not something they want to do. If you'd like to draw on some humor, you could tell them you're developing a new superpower.

They may witness how the benefits show in your health and behavior. Who knows? Maybe they will feel inspired to start meditating themselves.

COMMON CHALLENGES

The first step is to check our expectations. Most of us arrive at meditation with expectations for what it will feel like and what it will look like. We might have an image in our mind of someone sitting on a cushion looking peaceful. There may be a belief that this meditator's mind is completely quiet and free of thoughts. When the average person starts to meditate, one of the first things they notice is a busy mind and numerous distractions.

Common challenges faced by meditators fit on a short but formidable list. Because the challenges are so common, it can be helpful to know what they are. Meditators report frustrations like impatience, restlessness, boredom, sleepiness, doubt, discomfort, and self-criticism, among others. If you experience any of them, it doesn't mean you are meditating wrong. It means you are human.

Am I Meditating Yet?

The following are common questions many meditators have. Even experienced meditators wonder about some of these things.

When will I start to feel better?

Sometimes we will notice immediate benefits, like greater ease in the body or mind. When it comes to chronic stress, it is better to consider that the benefits are cumulative and you will notice them over time.

How do I know if I'm meditating and not just sitting there?

At any point while meditating, you can check in and see where you are regarding any of these phases: (1) You have chosen to be mindfully aware. (2) You are mindfully observing your moment-to-moment experiences. (Categories of experience you might be noticing are thoughts, emotions, impulses, or sensory information like body sensations or sounds.) (3) When you are recognizing distractions, you are simply noting the distractions and coming back to being mindfully aware.

If my mind isn't quiet when I meditate, am I doing it wrong?

Awareness of what's on your mind is part of the meditation experience. Even if it's just a whisper of thinking in the background, it's very common and natural to still be aware of thinking. Trying to suppress thoughts or control the mind usually just leads to tension and frustration.

Am I supposed to think?

Meditation doesn't require much mental activity, which is why it can be so calming. After choosing to be mindfully aware, our response to distractions that arise is based as much on attitude and intention as it is mental noting. You may still notice thinking, or become lost in thought, but the response can be as simple as refocusing attention on the breath or other instructions in the meditation.

What if I fall asleep?

If you fall asleep while meditating, when you wake up, simply notice that you drifted off and return to meditating—no judgment. If you find you're in that drowsy place between sleep and full wakefulness, a mindful response could be to create alertness by opening your eyes, lifting your chin so your head isn't slumped toward your chest, sitting up straighter, or even standing up.

What's the best meditation position?

The best position is one that allows you to be relaxed yet alert for a period of stillness and concentration and the one you will actually practice or use—which may even be lying down. There's no need to sit on the floor with your legs crossed. In MBSR classes, we sit in chairs where, ideally, our feet are on the floor and our backs are straight without being rigid. The hands are placed in the lap. Some find that placing a cushion on one's lap supports the arms in a way that relieves strain in the neck and shoulders.

Do I have to sit?

Sitting is helpful because it's easier to stay alert. Other positions are also a possibility. For example, you can lie down or even stand if that works best for your body. It's best to decide on a posture at the beginning of the meditation and then stick with it for the entire meditation session.

Do I need to wear special clothes, light candles, or burn incense?

For clothing, just being comfortable is most important. There's no need to light candles or burn incense, even though we may have seen pictures of this or know people who do. If you like candles or incense, one of the reasons to use them is to consciously set meditation apart from other types of activities. I have a friend who likes to light a stick of incense and then meditate with it until it is done burning.

What if it hurts to sit or I feel uncomfortable?

If sitting is not right for your body or you start to experience extreme pain, you can choose a different position or choose to meditate another time. That said, it's not uncommon to feel various kinds of discomfort while meditating. Whether your foot falls asleep, you get an itch, or you feel very fidgety, before adjusting your posture, use the "six-second rule": Pause and observe the experience for about six seconds. You may discover that thoughts and emotions contribute more to the discomfort than the position of your body.

What if I have chronic pain?

Mindfulness meditation also can help lower the impact of stress on pain and help us learn ways of responding to pain in the moment that can carry over into other times when we experience distress. Although it's not ideal to meditate when we are feeling challenged by pain, this could be a reason to do it for those who experience chronic pain.

Can I make my anxiety go away with meditation?

Some people report that their anxiety goes away when they meditate, but this usually happens after they have been meditating long enough to develop the kinds of skills described earlier in "Cognitive Behavioral Techniques" (page 8) or "The Attitudes of Mindfulness" (page 10). You might even notice anxiety a bit more in the beginning because you're intentionally paying attention. Over time, however, clinical evidence shows a significant reduction in anxiety and improved quality of life. It's important to remember that it's okay to feel anxiety while you are meditating. It doesn't mean you are doing it wrong. The body and mind still register the benefits, and these add up.

What if my mind wanders?

Mind wandering is not a problem. It is simply an aspect of being aware and having a mind. After all, it is the mind's job to think thoughts; it's our job to notice those thoughts and be able to witness them, rather than get drawn in or swept away by them. Just note what is on your mind, and return to your chosen focus.

When is the best time to practice?

Some people find morning best, because once the day gets started, schedules can be less predictable. At night, meditation can help us wind down, but we might find that we are tired in a way that makes it hard to concentrate or even stay awake. In my own case, I may do shorter meditations in the morning but have time for longer ones in the afternoon. That is also when the lull in my energy level supports settling down for some meditation. Over time, you'll find what works best for you.

How much time do I need?

Shorter sessions may be easier to fit into your day. Longer meditations give the mind and body more time to settle. We do not have scientific data on an optimal amount of time for meditation. Be careful not to raise the bar too high for yourself or judge yourself for the time you spend. Any amount of time spent meditating is beneficial.

Do I need a timer?

Using a timer can be helpful because then you don't have to watch the clock. At the beginning of the meditation, decide how long you will do it and keep to it. Most people will meditate longer if they use a timer.

Can I meditate while walking or running?

With activities that involve a lot of repetitive movement, technically one could concentrate on movement, counting, or the breath. The key is to notice when the mind has wandered and bring it back to your chosen focus. Generally, the more movement, the more active our mind. Walking meditation is done very slowly, so it's easier to focus, and distractions are limited.

Do I have to meditate every day?

Daily meditation—of whatever length of time—is optimal, but do what is best for you. Shorter meditations done every day, rather than a long one once a week, are more likely to become a habit and help you build some momentum as you develop your skills. Experiencing the benefits every day may also help keep you inspired. Remember, the benefits are cumulative.

A Peaceful Part of Your Day

Our routines exist within the landscape of our lives and all the other activities that happen as we move through our days. The following reflection can help form a meditation routine that meets your needs and fits your lifestyle. Even when a routine looks great on paper, if you can't connect with it physically and get yourself to do it, it probably won't stick. Meditate with the guidance of these reflections and you'll soon find yourself with a meditation routine that blends easily with all the other things you do! Return to this reflection regularly and make any changes necessary.

For this reflection, let yourself glance at the book from time to time to stay centered on the questions.

1. Dedicate time to reflect on your needs for meditation and get clear on your "why." Consider how your day affects you physically, starting with the morning.

2. Important: Recall what you like about meditation. Be specific, and base this on experience, not just ideas.

3. What kind of meditation(s) do you currently enjoy the most (or think you enjoy the most)?

4. What is your attention span like these days? Are you mentally fatigued or very distracted?

5. What types of things get in the way of regular meditation for you? For instance, responsibilities, the needs of others, your energy level, convenience, environment, and so on. Note that these are all normal aspects of life and being a meditator.

6. How much time do you realistically have for meditation?

7. Identify the place you will routinely do your meditation and the time of day when you are more likely to do it.

8. Pair your chosen kind of meditation with another activity you already do routinely so they become connected.

9. In your mind, come up with a plan and later write it down. In a week or so, revisit it and make any changes necessary. Revisit this reflection from time to time so you can refine your plan.

Calm the Mind

Contemporary research reveals that meditations like the ones that follow benefit the mind and body in ways that lead to an overall sense of relief or peace. They also help build foundational skills that support all the other meditations in this book. These are skills like learning to bring the mind back when it wanders, staying focused on the breath, and practicing with the cognitive behavioral techniques and attitudes of mindfulness described earlier.

Don't worry if you don't feel calm while you're doing these meditations. The benefits still register and add up. Over time, you may find you have favorites. They are all equally valuable as you continue to learn, grow, and become healthier through the stress reduction they offer.

Just This Breath

Moments of clarity and calm are as close as your next breath. Mindfulness of breathing is one of the oldest meditation practices, dating back thousands of years. Because of its simplicity, this type of meditation is referred to as a serenity practice. Since the mind has an endless number of things to pay attention to, we offer it just one thing, so it doesn't have to choose.

🕐 Start with 3 minutes, then move up to 5, 10, 15, 20—up to 45 minutes.

1. Choose an amount of time and set a timer.

2. Wherever you are, the important thing is mindset. Let yours be one of giving yourself space in your day, whether sitting or lying down. This meditation can be done anywhere, and conditions do not need to be perfect.

3. Take a moment of pause in your day.

4. Find a place to sit comfortably, with an attitude of relaxed alertness.

5. Allow the eyes to gently close.

6. Gathering your attention, bring it to focus on the fact that you are breathing.

7. There's no right way to breathe—just awareness of breathing is enough.

8. You might notice the rising and falling of the chest, feel the air flowing in and out of your nose, or observe the rising and falling of your abdomen. Simply sense the breath and let yourself be.

9. Notice where you feel the breath most vividly, and keep bringing attention back to this spot when you realize it has drifted elsewhere.

10. There's no need to go looking for the breath. Simply feel the breath coming and going. It's that simple. Just let yourself be.

Let Awareness Find You

We are always aware; we're mostly just not aware of being aware. General categories are thoughts, feelings, sensations, sounds—anything that you are perceiving in the "right now." This meditation has less structure than some. It can be good when you have had prior activities in your day that have required a great deal of focus. This is an opportunity to relax your attention and just let yourself be.

A sitting posture is ideal for this meditation, because if helps foster alertness, but you may also lie down or even walk slowly a few paces, back and forth, while doing this.

🕐 Start with 3 minutes, then move up to 5, 10, 15, 20—up to 45 minutes.

1. Find a place to sit comfortably, with an attitude of relaxed alertness.

2. Allow the eyes to gently close.

3. Start with using the breath as an anchor for your attention.

4. After staying with the breath for a while and developing some concentration, you can let go of the anchor and simply sit with awareness.

5. There will likely be awareness of thoughts, but what else? Sounds? Sensations? Mindfulness is big enough to hold anything and everything.

6. Just sit with awareness and let yourself be.

7. If you find your mind drifting, focus on your breath to help you stay connected.

8. Awareness is always here.

9. There's no need to control the mind. Just let yourself be.

3. Relaxed Alertness

When we're stressed, sometimes it can feel like we're experiencing decision overload. During meditation, even noticing thoughts can feel a little like sorting through the mail, as though we're supposed to do something with them. During meditation, there's a way to meet our thoughts that takes very little effort. A very simple acknowledgment of "thinking" can be enough. Here's how it can go.

🕐 15 minutes

1. Make a mindful transition to sitting comfortably in a way that supports a relaxed alertness.
2. Close your eyes or fix your gaze softly on a single object.
3. Turn your attention inward.
4. Consciously gather your attention and bring it to rest on the breath.
5. Use the breath as a resting place for your attention.
6. Continue breathing mindfully. When you start to notice thoughts, there's no need to put them anywhere or do anything about them, just mentally note "thinking."
7. The breath remains the primary anchor for attention. After noting "thinking," come back to the breath each time.
8. Some thoughts may feel as though they have greater priority; for these, too, just note "thinking."
9. Be willing to drop a thought, even the ones that seem more important than others.
10. Recognize that you are giving yourself a chance to let go of processing, deciding, planning, rehearsing, or any number of things we tend to do when we think.
11. Just let yourself be.

Creating Space for Insight

Processing, or reviewing, information is a function we depend on in daily life. When we start to witness this process during meditation, it is not a problem. We are just sitting ringside with a view of the inner working of our own mind. The practice here is to trust that this process can continue in the background, while we invite our attention to rest in the foreground. We can take a break from monitoring our thoughts.

🕐 10 minutes

1. Give yourself a break from your activities and find a comfortable place to sit.

2. When ready, bring your attention to rest on the breath.

3. Let yourself be, paying attention to the breath as it flows.

4. You may notice specific sensations related to the air flowing through the nostrils or movement of the chest or abdomen.

5. As thoughts arise in awareness and get your attention, just think "not now," and come back to the breath. After noting "not now," turn your attention back to awareness of breathing.

6. Continue breathing mindfully. You might even notice that some ways of breathing feel better to you. It's okay to change the way you breathe; the main thing is that when you become aware of thoughts, think "not now" and come back to the breath.

7. If other distractions arise, also note "not now," and come back to your breath again.

8. Let yourself be, resting with awareness of the breath in the foreground, while thoughts stay in the background.

5. Planting the Seeds of Calm

The concept of "planting the seeds of mindfulness" helps support an attitude of acceptance and trust that this is a process that needs to unfold naturally. One can't force a garden to grow, just as we can't force the mind to be calm. We just tend it as best we can and honor that we are doing this for our maximum interest in the long term, even if things are uncomfortable or unsatisfying right now. Each time we recognize we are trying to control the growing of the seeds, we begin again. The calm doesn't generally happen all at once, and it doesn't have to.

🕐 12 minutes

1. As with the other meditations for calm, find a relatively comfortable position that supports alertness. Many people find sitting to be the most accessible. Do what's right for you.

2. Recognize the fact that you are breathing.

3. Notice where you feel the breath most vividly. Breathe in with awareness of breathing in. Breathe out with awareness of breathing out.

4. When the mind wanders, bring it back to the breath.

5. If any sense of frustration or desire to control your experience arises, recall that all that's required is planting the seeds of calm with your intentions.

6. Let yourself be. You support your meditation practice with this attitude, and your meditation supports you. This attitude of acceptance can be the whole of the practice, no matter what distractions arise. Plant the seeds of calm, one moment at a time, one breath at a time.

Riding the Waves
of the Breath

The concept of waves on the ocean can be a great metaphor within meditation practice. Waves are a part of the ocean in the same way our moods are part of having a human mind. Consider the conditions at sea: The waters reflect the wind, weather, and tides. A perspective that the weather is a temporary condition can support us long after the meditation is over.

🕐 10 minutes (Use a timer.)

1. Find a comfortable meditation posture.

2. Allow your eyes to gently close, turning your attention inward.

3. Take a moment to check in with yourself as though getting an internal weather report. What are the conditions? Overcast with a chance of rain? A sky full of thunder? Partly cloudy? Scorching hot?

4. As you breathe, note the chest or belly rising and falling, like waves in the ocean. Some waves are bigger. Some are smaller. Just notice the conditions at hand.

5. When thoughts arise, consider them aspects of the weather, letting them be.

6. Stay with the breath, feeling the waves of the breath as they rise and fall.

7. When the timer goes off, check in with yourself for another weather report. Consider that the weather—even with its storms—is a temporary condition and a natural part of life.

7. Cultivating Inner Kindness

The practice of active goodwill, toward yourself and others, is often called "loving-kindness" meditation. Also known as metta practice in the ancient Pali language, this meditation dates to around 800 BCE. There is no right way to feel during loving-kindness meditation. The aim is to cultivate the conditions for these qualities to develop. We do this to help release the knots of tension and stress that arise when life or our inner conditions do not feel so kind.

🕐 15 minutes

1. Sit or lie in a comfortable position, with the eyes gently closed.

2. Recall a person in each of the following categories (or just stay with the easiest one):

   - Familiar stranger (someone you see often but don't know well—for example, a cashier or perhaps a neighbor)
   - Person "easy to love" (for example, a good friend)
   - Yourself
   - Someone *slightly* more challenging—don't raise the bar too high (for example, someone you know who annoys you mildly)

3. In your mind, think:

   - "May you (or I or we) be safe and protected from inner and outer harm."
   - "May you (or I or we) be peaceful."
   - "May you (or I or we) live with ease and with kindness."
   - You can simplify this further by noting only single words: "safe," "peace," "ease," "kindness."

A Heart of Wisdom: Gratitude Meditation

When things are going well, thoughts of gratitude are often more accessible. When we feel stressed, this notion is harder earned. Yet during difficult times, we can practice cultivating gratitude as a kind of formal meditation practice. For me, gratitude practice is particularly helpful during periods of grief. At times of loss, recognizing the good in life can generate a shift in perspective that reminds us of what we have. Students I've worked with who have chosen this for an evening meditation have reported its benefits in gaining perspective before falling asleep at night.

🕐 For stress, spend at least 5 to 10 minutes with this meditation. If you go longer, the paced breathing gives physical stress more time to ease.

1. Allow for time and space in your day or night to focus on this practice.

2. Let mindfulness of breathing be the focus of this meditation.

3. Gather your attention to focus on the breath.

4. As you settle into the meditation, take a slightly deeper breath in.

5. At the top of the inhale, pause. Hold the breath for a few seconds before breathing out.

6. Repeat the slow, deep inhale, pause, and then a long, slow exhale.

7. Continue breathing this way for three or four more breaths, or until you feel the body begin to calm.

8. When ready, recall something for which you're grateful. It could be something very profound or something very simple and mundane.

9. As you reflect with gratitude, stay with the breath. This will anchor your attention and help the body stay calm.

10. When the mind drifts and you recognize that it's drifted, bring your attention back to gratitude.

Self-Compassion Meditation

Several years ago, an extremely stressed student called me to say that the mindfulness was not helping with her stress. She was hoping there was a technique to use when her stress was "really, really" bad—had I perhaps forgotten to mention it in class? As we spoke, I learned that her child was facing a difficult surgery and she was feeling paralyzed with fear and worry. Because there was nothing she could do, she felt angry and sad, and her nights were sleepless. When we are suffering, especially with self-criticism, sometimes kindness is the only answer.

🕐 20 minutes; this gives the body and nervous system some time to settle and to incline the mind toward self-compassion.

1. Allow yourself to pause and become mindful of the way that you are feeling stressed, that you are suffering, that this experience hurts.

2. Consider that right now, and in all of history, there are people who feel or have felt exactly as you do right now. You are not alone with this. Take solace in knowing others know or have known this feeling, too.

3. If you wish, place a hand on your chest or find another physical gesture that embodies self-connection.

4. Offer yourself a supportive or comforting phrase like "I'm doing the best I can" or "I forgive myself," or any thoughts of goodwill that feel authentic to you. You can even picture yourself at some point in the future, feeling loved or happy or at ease.

5. Continue offering these thoughts or this gesture of goodwill toward yourself, envisioning yourself free of suffering. You can accompany it with awareness of breath.

Connect to Serenity

The origins of this meditation come from a meditation for tranquility that goes back to around 800 BCE. It may help you get a little space from habitual thought patterns that can influence stress and thus foster greater tranquility. This is to simply recognize what's on your mind, while allowing the breath to be front and center in awareness. When there's a choice between thought and breath, simply prefer the breath. When the meditation ends, we can still allow ourselves to "prefer the breath" to maintain a thread of serenity throughout all our activities.

🕐 Start with 3 minutes, then move up to 5, 10, 15, 20—up to 45 minutes.

1. Take a little time to settle in. Just for now, put the day or night on pause.

2. Allow yourself to be, just as you are.

3. Take some long, slow breaths, and, with each exhale, allow your shoulders to drop.

4. Breathe in a way that feels good to you. There is no need for judgment or to make the breath a project.

5. Breathe in with awareness of breathing in; breathe out with awareness of breathing out. Allow one breath to follow the next.

6. At some point, you'll start to become aware of what's on your mind. Perhaps there are thoughts that represent things going on in daily life. Perhaps your thoughts drift to things that are important to you—your needs, your dreams, your plans.

7. Without any judgment whatsoever, allow them to be. There is nothing to do or undo.

8. If a strong thought stream comes along and you get carried along with it, add a simple mental note: "Not now."

9. Give yourself over to the breath. Breathe in with awareness of breathing in, and breathe out with awareness of breathing out.

Calm the Body

Through mindfulness, we can learn to befriend our bodies, so the mind-body connection becomes an ally for coping with stress. Body awareness affords the mind a place to rest, rather than becoming lost in thought. This is also where we feel our own aliveness, receive valuable information about our needs and feelings, and create a sense of connection that can lead to positive ways of coping, instead of living on autopilot.

The mindful embodiment we cultivate during meditation can extend beyond the meditation session and support us through all our waking moments, even when we're not thinking about being mindful. Mindfulness meditation enlarges our capacity to be aware, to show up for ourselves, to cultivate unconditional acceptance, and to give ourselves time to *just be*.

Body Scan

Mindfulness includes the body. We can embody the body, appreciate the body, and rest in awareness. Allow it to be experienced the way it is, without descriptions, without adding a story to it. This is also a meditation where we can practice letting go of judgments about our body and put out the welcome mat for self-compassion and acceptance. When we're stressed, we might want to avoid feeling our body, but uniting body and mind restores balance. The body scan meditation helps you be more mindfully responsive to your body's feedback, especially during stressful times.

🕐 20 minutes

1. Find a place where you can be undisturbed.
2. Lie down if you can, or find a position that supports relaxed alertness.
3. When you're ready, allow the eyes to gently close.
4. Take some time for mindful breathing. While doing the body scan, you can use it as an additional anchor for staying focused and aware.
5. Move your attention slowly through your body, noting sensations such as warmth, coolness, lightness, heaviness, tingling, or pressure. Picture these areas lighting up as you move along.
6. If there are thoughts, acknowledge them as thoughts, then come back to the body. Let go of self-judgment.
7. As you reach the end of the meditation, rest in awareness and let yourself be.

Tip: It isn't important to feel a certain way while you are doing the body scan, but rather to be aware of what you are noticing—even if it's the absence of sensations.

The Breath of Life:
A Deep Breathing Meditation

Deep breathing can be very relaxing. It is one way we can regulate our nervous system. We can calm a racing heart, regulate anxiety, and guide an agitated mind and body toward a state of calm.

🕐 10 minutes

1. Take these 10 minutes to give yourself some time and attention, to just be.

2. If possible, lie down so that you don't have to put any effort into staying upright.

3. Allow the arms to rest alongside your body.

4. Feel the support of the floor or wherever you are. Give your weight over to it, supported by gravity.

5. Start to take long, slow breaths, equal on the in and out: A long, slow breath in, followed by a long, slow breath out. You don't have to think of all the future breaths that are going to be breathed, just the one that's happening right now.

6. As you breathe, take deep breaths as though breathing all the way down into the bottom of your lungs.

7. Allow for a three-dimensional expansion of the lung region. Notice if you feel the breath even in the back of your body.

8. Long, slow breath in. Long, slow breath out.

9. Let yourself be.

Feeling Supported during Stress

One metaphor in particular helps me understand the way meditation gradually makes us calmer: when still, muddy water or cloudy apple juice becomes clearer. This same process happens with the development of calm in the body. We just need a little time to be still, so our stressed nervous system can settle on its own. We can create the right conditions for this to happen, and the rest takes care of itself.

🕐 20 minutes

1. Take a lying position in your location of choice. Feel the support of the surface beneath you, recognizing it is holding your entire weight, so that you can start to relax. Let this support truly register. It can take on your full weight.

2. Check in with your body. Notice if there are areas of tension anywhere. Also notice where there may be areas with no tension. There's no need to force relaxation; we're putting a welcome mat out for it to arise.

3. Start breathing slowly and regularly, and continue breathing in this way for the rest of the meditation.

4. Again, feel the support of the surface beneath your body.

5. With each exhale, invite your body to relax.

6. As you recognize tension in your body, with each exhale, invite any contracted muscles to soften, to release, to become more relaxed.

7. Turn attention again to the support of where you are lying, noticing that you are supported both physically and metaphorically. Imagine you are becoming heavier, supported by gravity.

8. The breath and body can be an anchor for attention, while you use the rhythmic flow of the breath to help you relax more deeply. Breathe evenly, slowly, and deeply.

9. If there are pleasant sensations in the body, acknowledge them, noticing their fullness and detail.

10. If you would like to add a mental note, with each exhale, think "relax." Although we are not trying to force the body to relax, we can put out an invitation for this to happen, even if we don't feel it while we're doing it.

11. "Relax" and let be for as long as you'd like.

Progressive Relaxation

Whereas the Body Scan meditation (see page 36) fosters being present to our experience of the body and just letting ourselves be, the Progressive Relaxation technique aims to relax our muscles in a way that many find very soothing. It unites our mental intention with gently contracting, and then releasing, each region of the body sequentially. Many have found this to be a great way to fall asleep at night.

🕐 20 to 30 minutes

1. Take a lying position in the location of your choice. Whatever your location and time of day or night, allow your surroundings to register. With eyes open, acknowledge your environs, perhaps also noticing a sense of quiet, or any background noise.

2. Bring attention to body and breath. As with the other meditations, the breath can serve as your go-to anchor for attention when the mind becomes active, distracted, or agitated.

3. Feel the support of the surface beneath you, recognizing it is supporting your entire weight so that you can start to relax. Feel that support and let it register.

4. Breathe evenly on the in and out. For right now, this is all that needs to be done. You may notice that with the inhale, the breathing muscles tighten slightly, and with the release of air, they relax. Stay with the breath this way. Feel the tightening of the chest muscles with the inhale, pause, and with the release of air, feel the muscles of the chest relax. Stay with this for 5 to 10 cycles of the breath (your choice).

5. Now shift attention to your hands, arms, and shoulders. As you inhale, make the hands into tight fists and tighten the muscles of the arms. Pause at the top of the inhale, and then with the exhale, allow the muscles of the hands and arms to relax. Feel the sensations of the tension being released.

6. Next, shift attention to the legs and feet. With an inhale, tighten the muscles of the legs and feet, perhaps pointing the toes. At the top of the inhale, pause for a moment, holding the contraction. Then exhale, letting go. Feel the sensations of letting go as you release the tension. Notice any pleasant sensations: warmth, tingling, lightness, or heaviness—whatever arises in awareness. If there is still tension elsewhere in the body, recognize any sensations of ease or relaxation.

7. Bring awareness to the back of your torso, up into your shoulders and neck. With these areas as well, tighten as you inhale, intentionally contracting your muscles. Pause, holding the breath and the constricted areas, then release and let go.

8. Turn your attention to the sensations in your face. Inhale, contracting the muscles of the face, even the muscles you don't usually recognize. Pause as you hold the breath and the contracted muscles. Then exhale, feeling the release of tension and the sensations that follow.

9. Turn attention to the entire body. Recognize how the body is feeling. There may be pleasant sensations, but perhaps also some pockets of tension remaining. While inhaling, contract the muscles of the entire body: feet, legs and hips, abdomen and chest area, hands and arms, back, shoulders, and neck and face. Pause. And release.

10. Rest in awareness and let yourself be.

Integrating Peace through Sensory Clarity

Throughout the body, we have a direct connection to our own aliveness. We experience this through all of our senses. When we are lost in stress reactivity, it's easy for the story unfolding in our lives to take up all our attention. With this meditation, just experience the present moment through your senses. Feel your own aliveness and let yourself be for a while.

🕐 5 to 10 minutes per category of attention (breath, body, sound, etc.)

1. Start either lying down or sitting in a way that is balanced, relaxed, and alert.

2. Anchor your attention with awareness of the breath. Breathe slowly and deeply to help you start slowing down. As you continue to settle, you can breathe in whatever way feels most natural.

3. When ready, invite awareness of your body's sensations. Just notice what arises. Perhaps warmth or coolness, lightness or heaviness, tingling, pressure. Some sensations may seem still; others may seem to move. Some are deep; some are shallow.

4. After a period of time, turn your attention to awareness of sound. Listening with awareness, observe how the ears simply receive sound. Notice sounds nearby and sounds far away, sounds within and outside the room.

5. We experience the present moment through our senses. Recognize other sensory information arising, like any sense of taste or your visual experience.

6. If you're aware of thoughts, you might also notice that thoughts have a visual component through imagery, or sound through imagined speech.

7. See what happens when you give yourself a moment to sit in pure awareness. Remain open to whatever arises.

8. If you need an additional attention anchor, use the breath. Otherwise, continue letting your attention rest in awareness, open to changing sensations, sounds, visual phenomena, or taste.

9. When thoughts arise, be willing to drop the thought and come back to sensory awareness.

10. Feel yourself supported by the surface beneath you.

11. Let yourself be.

Calm Mountain:
Standing Meditation

One of the most flexible of meditation practices is standing meditation. It is highly portable and very practical. You can do it anywhere, whether standing at the microwave waiting for the timer to ring, standing in line at the grocery store, at home, work, or anywhere else.

🕐 2 to 10 minutes, depending on where you are

1. You can do this anywhere as a kind of informal practice, or choose a time and set a timer so that you don't need to watch the clock.

2. Stand with awareness of standing. This is called mountain pose in yoga, but you can think of it as just standing with awareness.

3. Think of lifting through the crown of the head, while feeling sensations in the feet. The legs are straight but the knees are slightly unlocked.

4. Gently shift the weight from side to side, sensing that you are moving slightly off balance, and then back to center.

5. Pause. Let yourself be.

6. Anchor your attention with body sensations, or the breath, or the shapes and colors of objects and spaces that are in your view. Mindfully listen to sound. All of these are options. You can choose where to put your attention, or just notice what arises in awareness.

7. If there are other people around (for instance, if you are standing in line somewhere), notice the activity while letting go of judgments.

8. Let yourself be, for as long as you like or until the timer goes off.

The Path to Serenity: Walking Meditation

There are a variety of ways to practice walking meditation. The two options described here draw on focused attention and body awareness. The simpler our focus and the slower our pace, the easier it is for the mind to settle and calm. Option 1 involves a focus on the breath, and Option 2 draws on sensations in the feet. In meditation #44 (see page 87), the focus is more on awareness of the environment, and you can walk faster. Give them all a try.

Option 1: Use the breath to stay anchored, connected, present, and aware while you walk. We're drawing on the breath for support the way we might use a guide rail for support. A part of awareness will stay with the body, a part with the surroundings. The mind may remain active to some extent. As with other meditations, if you notice you've become lost in thought, gently bring the mind back to awareness of the present.

Option 2: Note sensations in the feet as you walk. When you recognize the mind has wandered, come back to the sensations in the feet. If you'd like, add a mental note of "lifting" or "placing."

🕐 10 to 30 minutes (Use a timer.)

1. Decide if you'll practice Option 1 or Option 2, and set a timer so that you don't need to watch the clock.

2. Find a space that gives you room for a path of about 10 to 15 paces. It doesn't really matter where you do it, be it indoors, as in a hallway, bedroom, motel room, or office, or outdoors, as in your yard, on the porch, in a park or parking lot. Identify the beginning and end of the path. Select a space where you feel safe.

3. Standing at the beginning of your path, acknowledge where you are as well as a sense of your own body.

(continues)

4. Become aware of the breath. Stay in touch with the breath or sensations in the feet.

5. Begin walking. You don't have to walk at any special speed. Just mindfully walk, staying connected to the breath or sensations in the feet.

6. You will probably become aware of the general environment, including the visual elements or sounds. Keep coming back to either the breath or sensations in the feet.

7. Aim to stay mindfully present for the full duration of the walking path. If your mind is active, gently bring yourself back to the sensations each time.

8. Stay mindfully present as you walk.

9. When you get to the end of your path, pause, mindfully turn, and go back the other direction. If you're feeling unfocused or agitated, take a little extra time to pause and reconnect with yourself and the earth before returning down the path.

10. Finish by simply standing. Awareness of the body. Of surroundings. Acknowledge what's here. Check in with yourself: body, mind, emotions. Ask yourself if there is anything particularly valuable that you'd like to remember for future practice.

Tip: Instead of noticing sensations in the feet, you could alternatively pay attention to sensations of motion while in a chair or mindfully move a different body region. For example, turn the hands palms up, then palms down repetitively, or slowly gaze upward, then downward.

Releasing Stress through Mindful Movement

Stress is often reflected in the body with an experience of being tense or contracted. For many of us, when we're not in "fight or flight" mode, we might embody a freeze response. Becoming very still can also be a way of managing emotions. Other times, we are so caught in the mental dramas at hand that we forget about our bodies entirely. Mindful movement can help calm our bodies. On the simplest level it involves tuning in to the body and breath while we gently stretch.

🕐 10 minutes

1. Find a stable position, either sitting or standing. Shift your weight from side to side and become aware of your center.

2. Find a spot to hold your gaze while bringing attention to a sense of your spine. Think of rooting down through the tailbone as you extend the spine upward. You can imagine making space between the vertebrae, the bones of the spinal column.

3. Take some long, slow breaths here; with each exhale, imagine there are heavy wings attached to your shoulder blades. Feel your feet in contact with the floor.

4. When ready, bring the arms overhead in a full body stretch. If you'd like, interlace the fingers and press your palms up to face the ceiling.

5. As you come back to center, bring your arms back to your sides and let your hands come to rest gently in your lap.

6. Do another full body stretch. This time extend a little higher with one of the arms and lean gently toward the other side. You can think of this as though you're making extra space between your hip bone and the lower ribs. Feel the stretch in your side.

(continues)

7. Repeat on the other side, then come back to center and repeat once more on each side.

8. With arms at your side, come forward into a forward bend. Start by letting the head come toward the chest, then go over, vertebra by vertebra, unstacking the spine.

9. When you reach the full forward bend that suits your body, stay awhile, if you'd like, before gently coming up, restacking the vertebrae of the spine.

10. When you are back to where you started, pause and take several long, slow breaths, letting yourself be.

11. Finish with a full body stretch. Turn attention to awareness of the body sitting or standing. Rest in this awareness.

Barnes & Noble Booksellers #2194

96 Derby Street Suite 300
Hingham, MA 02043
781-749-3319

STR:2194 REG:008 TRN:0801 CSHR:Patrick F

Power of Now: A Guide to Spiritual Enlig
9781577314806   T1
    (1 @ 17.00)   17.00
Mindfulness Meditations for Stress: 100
9781647399016   T1
    (1 @ 16.99)   16.99
Subtotal   33.99
Sales Tax T1 (6.250%)   2.12
TOTAL   36.11
MASTERCARD DEBIT   36.11
Card#: XXXXXXXXXXXXX5016

Application Label: US Debit
AID: a0000000042203
PIN Verified
TVR: 8000048000
TSI: 6800

A MEMBER WOULD HAVE SAVED   3.40

Connect with us on Social!

Facebook - @bhingham
Instagram- @bhingham
Twitter- @BNHingham

055.01C   08/11/2021 01:33PM

Third Free offer are available for exchange only, unless all items purchased as part of the offer are returned, in which case such items are available for a refund (in 30 days). Exchanges of the items sold at no cost are available only for items of equal or lesser value than the original cost of such item.

Opened music CDs, DVDs, vinyl records, electronics, toys/games, and audio books may not be returned, and can be exchanged only for the same product and only if defective. NOOKs purchased from other retailers or sellers are returnable only to the retailer or seller from which they were purchased pursuant to such retailer's or seller's return policy. Magazines, newspapers, eBooks, digital downloads, and used books are not returnable or exchangeable. Defective NOOKs may be exchanged at the store in accordance with the applicable warranty.

Returns or exchanges will not be permitted (i) after 30 days or without receipt or (ii) for product not carried by Barnes & Noble.com, (iii) for purchases made with a check less than 7 days prior to the date of return.

Policy on receipt may appear in two sections.

Return Policy

With a sales receipt or Barnes & Noble.com packing slip, a full refund in the original form of payment will be issued from any Barnes & Noble Booksellers store for returns of new and unread books, and unopened and undamaged music CDs, DVDs, vinyl records, electronics, toys/games and audio books made within 30 days of purchase from a Barnes & Noble Booksellers store or Barnes & Noble.com with the below exceptions:

Undamaged NOOKs purchased from any Barnes & Noble Booksellers store or from Barnes & Noble.com may be returned within 14 days when accompanied with a sales receipt or with a Barnes & Noble.com packing slip or may be exchanged within 30 days with a gift receipt.

A store credit for the purchase price will be issued (i) when a gift receipt is presented within 60 days of purchase, (ii) for all textbooks returns and exchanges, or (iii) when the original tender is PayPal.

Items purchased as part of a Buy One Get One or Buy Two, Get Third Free offer are available for exchange only, unless all items purchased as part of the offer are returned, in which case such items are available for a refund (in 30 days). Exchanges of the items sold at no cost are available only for items of equal or lesser value than the original cost of such item.

Opened music CDs, DVDs, vinyl records, electronics, toys/games, and audio books may not be returned, and can be exchanged only for the same product and only if defective. NOOKs purchased from other retailers or sellers are returnable only to the retailer or seller from which they were purchased pursuant to such retailer's or seller's return policy. Magazines, newspapers, eBooks, digital downloads, and used books are not returnable or exchangeable. Defective NOOKs may be exchanged at the store in accordance with the applicable warranty.

Returns or exchanges will not be permitted (i) after 30 days or without receipt or (ii) for product not carried by Barnes & Noble.com, (iii) for purchases made with a check less than 7 days prior to the date of return.

Policy on receipt may appear in two sections.

Return Policy

With a sales receipt or Barnes & Noble.com packing slip, a full refund in the original form of payment will be issued from any Barnes & Noble Booksellers store for returns of new and unread books, and unopened and undamaged music CDs, DVDs, vinyl records, electronics, toys/games and audio books made within 30 days of purchase from a Barnes & Noble Booksellers store or Barnes & Noble.com with the below exceptions:

Undamaged NOOKs purchased from any Barnes & Noble Booksellers store or from Barnes & Noble.com may be returned within 14 days when accompanied with a sales receipt or with a Barnes & Noble.com packing slip or may be exchanged within 30 days with a gift receipt.

A store credit for the purchase price will be issued (i) when a gift receipt is presented within 60 days of purchase, (ii) for all textbooks returns and exchanges, or (iii) when the original tender is PayPal.

Items purchased as part of a Buy One Get One or Buy Two, Get

Valid through 8/31/2021

Buy 1
Fresh Baked Cookie
Get 50% OFF a 2nd

Mix or Match any flavor

To redeem: Present this coupon in the Cafe.

C8V9R8C

Buy 1 Fresh Baked Cookie Get 50% OFF a 2nd:
Valid for Fresh Baked cookies only.
1 redemption per coupon.
Ask Cafe cashier for details.

Radiant Body Breathing

This meditation is based on a form of mindful movement that is known as qigong, which is similar to tai chi. It involves mindful movement and light visualization that aids with relaxation, easing the body and mind. I learned this practice from qigong teacher Teja Bell. You can adapt the movements for the needs of your body.

🕐 10 to 20 minutes

1. Stand mindfully.

2. Picture a clear mountain pool in front of you. Imagine it is filled with pure, clean, healing water.

3. With arms resting at your sides and palms facing upward, mindfully lift your arms up overhead and imagine you are gathering and scooping this pure, healing water up alongside you.

4. Then, turn the palms over, moving them through the space in front of your body, imagining the healing water is showering down your front.

5. Picture that your mental and physical stress is being cleared away.

6. Do this same movement several times, coordinating it with your breath: inhaling as the arms come up overhead, exhaling as they come down the center, clearing away the stress.

7. When you are ready, switch directions. This time scoop the pure, healing water up your front, palms up, showering it down your sides, palms down. Coordinate this, too, with the breath. Breathe in while scooping the water up your front. Exhale as it showers down alongside of you.

8. Continue these movements for as long as you'd like.

9. Finish by pausing and placing both palms over your abdomen, one resting on the other.

10. Breathe mindfully, enjoying the sensations of ease generated by the gentle movement and imagery.

The Lake

This meditation uses the metaphor of a lake to support relaxation. In MBSR classes, we frequently include this meditation during daylong retreats. It helps provide perspective that, no matter how stressful conditions are on the surface of a lake, below the surface one can find calm and quiet waters. Take a little time to rest, picturing this imagery.

🕐 10 to 15 minutes

1. Find a spot to lie down.

2. After you have found a comfortable position, check in with yourself and get an internal weather report. Is it windless or stormy? Raining or full of sun? Without judgment, imagine how things are for you. Perhaps your internal weather report reflects the stress in your life.

3. Now picture an image of a lake. This may be a lake you know in person, one you have seen in a photo, or one you have just made up. All are great options. Picture the surface of this lake. If it's a windless day, it may be as smooth as glass or a mirror, reflecting sky, clouds, trees, or whatever its surroundings.

4. Imagine the time of day for this lake. It could be dark or light. The sun could be out, or maybe the moon and a sky full of stars.

5. Map your internal weather conditions to the weather conditions of your lake. What happens to the surface of the water? Is it quiet? Are there ripples or waves? Perhaps there are large waves, even frothing.

6. Now, imagine going below the surface. Feel the water becoming calmer. Even if there's a storm raging on the surface, down below it is quiet, maybe even peaceful.

7. Consider your experience of your own life. Regardless of the conditions on the surface, what happens as you let your attention drop down, below the surface?

8. Imagine the floor of the lake. Is it flat or rocky? Deep or shallow? Whatever the surface, notice how the water of the lake is level, even if there are rocks below. All of these elements are just part of being a lake. Just as in our own lives, stress can be there, even while other things may still be okay on the surface.

9. Consider how the weather conditions—internal or external—are always temporary and part of life.

10. With this perspective, rest with awareness. If you wish, continue staying with the breath, breathing slowly and regularly.

PART II

Soothing the Stress Spectrum

The following 60 meditations support you as you encounter a wide range of daily stressors. Maybe it's the day all your plans go wrong. Perhaps you're dealing with chronic pain, or you want to target the stress related to big life events. These meditations aim to help you soothe yourself when you're tense, to gain perspective when you have a worried mind.

Rather than let stress build up, you can add these practices to your daily routine. You can also use them on the spot when life gets intense. Specifically, we'll cover four areas of the stress spectrum: Everyday Stress, Chronic Stress, Emotional Stress, and Big Life Events. Your body and mind will thank you for adding these mindfulness meditations into your daily self-care.

Everyday Stress

The average day is rarely average. We may start out thinking we know how things are going to go, but things don't always turn out according to plan. This is life—made up of an infinite number of moments. Bringing mindfulness to these moments, whether paying the bills, driving in traffic, or de-stressing while running late, can help us reclaim our lives amid the stressors so we can live all our moments fully.

In the midst of the busiest day or most anxious night, mindfulness meditation can help us recharge or replenish our energy, soothe feelings of agitation, or calm a racing mind. Through mindfulness, we can support ourselves with care and attention, even on a stressful day.

Waiting in
the Grocery Line

Our busy lives can make it seem as if there's no time for meditation, but the perfect meditation break can happen when doing something as ordinary as standing in line. When we'd rather be somewhere else, waiting in line can sometimes feel like a waste of our time. We miss out on so many moments when we get used to living that way. Cultivating mindfulness during informal meditation, like waiting in line, can have crossover benefits for all the moments that come afterward and contribute to stress management. No amount of time is too small, yet you can reclaim the moments, minutes, and hours of your life with this informal meditation practice.

🕐 3 to 10 minutes while waiting in line somewhere

1. Bring awareness to the fact that you are standing. Check in with how you're standing, and balance your weight evenly over both feet.

2. As an informal yoga pose, think of lifting through the crown of your head as you imagine rooting down through the floor, as though you were a tree.

3. Find an intentional spot for your gaze, and bring attention to focus on your breath. Spend some time mindful of breathing. When your mind jumps to analyzing, judging, evaluating, or any other type of experience, just note it and come back to the breath.

4. As the line moves forward, stay with your meditation. Step forward. Then pause once again. Come back to mountain pose. Breathe slowly and regularly.

5. By the time you reach the checkout, you will have reclaimed many minutes of meditation for yourself. Check in. Be sure to notice any benefit you feel so it can inspire you to practice this way again in the future.

Mealtime Meditation

As you get ready to eat, formally pause. Treat this interval as a mini meditation break. Whether you are eating by yourself or with others, mindfulness at mealtime can be a way to connect with yourself, perhaps others, and to be present for the meal you are eating. Eating can be both one of the most pleasurable things you do and a source of stress, or it may reflect the ways that you are stressed. Approaching a meal consciously doesn't have to be a complex or involved experience. Even one bite eaten mindfully can encompass the entirety of a meditation practice.

To practice with others, as you begin the meal you can suggest everyone try this together, for even just one bite. Children may be quite open to this kind of "game." A shared mindful meal can be tremendous for relationships.

🕐 2 to 30 minutes (Use a timer for a more "formal" meditation, or go without.)

1. As you sit down to eat, before you take a bite of anything, pause and turn your attention inward.

2. Consider that in a few moments, you'll be eating some food; what is outside of your body will soon be inside, providing nourishment.

3. Take a deep breath and let it out. Use mindful breathing to help you slow down and switch gears.

4. Check in with how you're feeling, especially noting your level of hunger or lack of hunger.

5. Note any emotions that are present now or were present earlier.

6. Notice if you are energized, fatigued, or somewhere in between.

7. Take a little time to consider the origins of this food. How did it make its way to you?

8. When ready, choose your first bite. Eat it slowly and mindfully. Savor flavors. Chew deliberately. When ready, swallow deliberately.

(continues)

9. After swallowing, pause. Sit with awareness of how you feel. What remains in your awareness?

10. One bite may be enough for you right now, or you can spend more time with this practice. At times you may want to eat an entire meal mindfully.

Mindfulness when You're Running Late

As we move faster, it's easy for the mind to also move fast. Let's say you're in traffic and there's suddenly gridlock. Or maybe you're racing around the house, madly trying to get out the door. Perhaps you're trying to get somewhere by a certain time. Possibly you cut it a little close and are even a little mad at yourself. As stress rises and we start to rush, it's as though we speed up inside, too. At this point, remind yourself that you're never late for the present moment.

🕐 1 to 30 minutes

1. Become mindfully aware of the fact that you're hurrying. Do this without judgment. There's no need to change your feelings in order to become mindful.

2. Let your breath be an anchor for your attention, even while you are rushing around.

3. Be fully present for what hurrying feels like.

4. Adopt a mindful attitude while hurrying. Be here for yourself with mindfulness. Hurrying on the inside won't help you get where you want to be any faster.

5. You may notice stress-like feelings in your body. That's okay—if you're hurrying, the stress reaction is temporarily giving you extra fuel to do so. Perhaps appreciate the fact that your body can do this.

6. Any amount of time you spend bringing mindfulness into a "hurrying" scenario will likely reduce the wear and tear of stress and help you come back into balance more consciously.

7. When the activity reaches its natural conclusion, reflect on how it made a difference for you and anything you would like to remember for a future time.

Simple Snacking

There's an activity that we sometimes do unconsciously, and that is snacking. We snack for more reasons than hunger. Sometimes we do so out of boredom; sometimes we do it because we are procrastinating or distracting ourselves from feelings. Sometimes we do it just because we enjoy food, and, if it's around, it's hard to resist. Whatever your relationship is to snacking, you can use mindfulness to "wake up" to the experience.

🕐 1 to 5 minutes

1. As you find yourself going for a snack, pause and check in with yourself.

2. Slowly breathing in fully, and then slowly breathing out fully, let yourself pause.

3. Whether standing or sitting, check in with your body and notice how you're feeling. How's your energy? Notice what's on your mind or your mental state.

4. Ask yourself if you have any unmet needs. Is there boredom or loneliness? Are you truly hungry? If so, what might satisfy it?

5. Let go of judgment, but ask yourself, "Could I care for myself in some way other than snacking"?

6. If you choose to eat your snack, be fully mindful of the experience. Notice flavor or the lack of flavor. Notice sounds, like crunching or noises related to wrappers or utensils or other sources. Visually take in the sight of your snack. If you are eating quickly, just note it. No need to change your pace, but you might decide you want to.

7. Bring mindfulness to all your senses as you eat. When you finish eating, pause again. Check in. Ask yourself if there is anything you would like to remember from this experience that may help you in the future.

Mindful Communication

"People stress" is one of the most difficult to endure because people don't tend to follow the scripts that *we* would choose for them. At work, home, or anyplace, there may be stressful things happening, but stress related to other people can make life feel a lot harder. This informal meditation will bring mindfulness into the realm of communication.

🕐 In the moment

1. Become mindful during a stressful communication experience.

2. Bring attention to rest on the flow of your breath as a way of staying anchored to the present.

3. As the other person is speaking, invite your full attention into being a listener.

4. When your mind jumps into planning what you're going to say or making assumptions about the person's meaning, bring it back to just listening. Give them your full attention.

5. Check in with yourself and read the stress in your body. Pounding heart? Palms sweaty? Mind racing? Any physical tension? These symptoms can point to what your needs are.

6. When you speak, do so in short sentences. Be willing to pause. Remember to breathe.

7. Unless something urgent needs to happen, consider that this conversation could be continued another time. Recognize when you have reached your limit.

8. Consider summarizing what you heard the other person say—even in just a few (one to three) words—so that they know you have been listening.

(continues)

9. Decide when it feels like the right time to stop or put a pause on the conversation.

10. After you finish, spend some time on your own with mindful breathing, and ask yourself what you might want to remember for a future time.

Transform Procrastination

We procrastinate for different reasons, yet no matter the reason, putting things off can add to our stress. Supporting ourselves through mindfulness can unblock our momentum. Although we might view procrastination in a negative light, self-understanding and mindfulness can help us move through procrastination so we can become even more efficient and productive. As with all forms of meditation, consciousness is key.

🕐 5 to 15 minutes (Use a timer.)

1. Take your seat (or lie down) and bring attention to your breath. Spend some time with mindful breathing.

2. The mind will likely wander; just notice where it goes. These thoughts could provide clues to your real priorities, conflicting needs, or creative ideas. Acknowledge them.

3. Each time you recognize that your mind has wandered, note "not right now" and come back to the breath. Be willing to drop a thought and come back to your breath.

4. When your concentration becomes stronger, picture in detail the focus of your procrastination. Visualize yourself engaged in the project. You may want to picture yourself completing it and the positive feelings you would have if you did.

5. If other thoughts or distractions arise, continue noting "not right now." Do this for the remainder of the meditation.

6. When the timer goes off, mindfully move forward into your day, knowing that you have set the stage for accomplishing your aim while being there for yourself. This attitude may accompany you as you approach your intended task.

A Mindful Start
to Your Workday

The start of the workday can set the tone for everything that follows. Done as a kind of daily ritual, this meditation can infuse your day with perspective and clarity. For added benefit, choose something that works with your routine so you can remember to do it each time you arrive at work, whatever "work" means to you.

🕐 1 to 2 minutes

1. At your place of work, designate a specific arriving activity as your base for mindfulness practice.

2. Just as you might prepare for sitting meditation, transition consciously.

3. Mindfully pause before sitting down or getting started with your work. Temporarily let go of what might happen when you get going again.

4. Standing or sitting, let all your momentum come to a full stop. Take a deep breath and drop your shoulders. Check in with your body.

5. Take between 3 and 10 mindful breaths as a deep inhale through your nose, and passively exhale through your mouth. Don't force the breath out; just relax as you feel the breath release.

6. If your eyes are closed, as you open them, do so slowly. Check in with your body. Note how you are feeling and your state of mind.

7. When you start moving again, stay with yourself for as long as that connection consciously remains in awareness. You can come back to it again and again.

Stress-Free Email

Mindfulness meditation for email problems! Who knew? This meditation will use a practice called "mindful investigation," an ally in mindfulness. Many people report inboxes with hundreds of unread emails. Even with a never-ending stream of email and a bottomless inbox, here's how to bring mindfulness to email management in a way that relieves stress. Center yourself in mindfulness with this practice.

🕐 5 to 10 minutes (Consider resetting the timer for each email.)

1. Wherever you respond to email, take a posture that is relaxed but alert.

2. Take some time to become centered with your breath.

3. When ready, open an email that you want to address. Scan through it, taking in the general content. There's no need to do anything else. Just read the email till the end.

4. Take your hands off the keyboard or put down your device. Turn back toward your meditation posture, centering yourself with the breath.

5. Keeping it simple, identify the top three things that need to be addressed in a response.

6. Pause and take a deep, refreshing breath. Give your brain this additional oxygen. Do a full body stretch, unfreezing any tension that has arisen.

7. When you are ready, return to the email and write a response, addressing the points you identified. (It may be that you need more time to accomplish a task, in which case you might simply acknowledge having received the email, note the items you will address and when you'll complete the task, and send it off.)

8. Reward yourself with another full body stretch or a positive phrase like "Well done!"

Mindful
Internet Browsing

How do you recognize when you've had enough online chatter and information? This is an informal meditation practice that can bring consciousness to an activity that for many of us is quite mindless. We leave ourselves without knowing it and get lost. It can be fun to become immersed online, but it's also easy to lose touch with our bodies, with our needs. By staying in touch, we can enjoy the benefits of going online while also recognizing when we've had enough. To make this a more formal meditation practice, use a timer.

🕐 5 minutes (Timer optional.)

1. Before going online, check in with yourself. Notice how you are feeling, on the level of body, mind, and general mood.

2. What need are you hoping to meet by going online right now? Common reasons are things like loneliness and boredom, or the need to accomplish a task, buy something, or connect socially.

3. Before continuing, ask yourself how you will recognize that your purpose of being online is concluded. How will you recognize that you have had enough or that your mission is complete?

4. When the timer goes off, ask yourself if the need you had for going online has been satisfied. If it has, ask yourself how you know for sure. Are you getting signals from your physical experience, or emotionally, that tell you, or is it because a task was completed? How do you feel?

5. Finally, how might this experience influence future choices you make about going online in a way that serves your greater well-being? Remember what you have learned for future inspiration.

Soothe Stress in Traffic

Out of all of the mundane stresses in life, traffic stress tops my list. There are so many things that make it anxiety producing. Although we have control over our vehicle, we can't control all those other fast (or slow) cars around us. If you add a few other nerve-racking elements like zipper merges, the weather, or running late, it's the perfect stress cocktail. Here's an informal meditation to soothe your stress while in traffic. Of course, do this with your eyes open and while you're still paying attention to the road.

🕐 5 to 30 minutes (whenever you're driving)

1. If you start to feel stressed while driving, use mindfulness to address your needs.

2. Ask yourself if there's anything you need to do to be safer, and let this be your first mindful response.

3. Bring awareness to a sense of your body, the support of the seat and the feel of the steering wheel.

4. Visually take in the car interior. Become aware of sounds.

5. To help you feel calmer, breathe slowly and regularly.

6. If music is on, try turning it off. Simplify. It can be so much simpler to drive in a quiet car.

7. If your mind is racing, use your breath to pace yourself. Traffic may be going fast, but a focus on regular breathing can help calm and clear your mind.

8. To regulate your emotions, keep breathing mindfully. If you're snapping at other drivers, try to recognize any assumptions going through your mind.

9. Calm any restlessness or agitation with a deep breath.

10. Recognize your environment; widen your perspective to outside your vehicle. Stay alert to changing conditions.

(continues)

11. Continue the practice for as long as you wish, knowing that mindfulness is helping you regulate stress while on your way safely to your destination.

Note: A version of this meditation can be done with any form of transportation. Whether going by subway, train, bus, bike, or skateboard, instead of "driving," "car," or "steering," think of terms that work better for your situation.

De-stress
While Paying Bills

We can de-stress while paying bills by inviting greater focus and calm. It may be hard to picture paying your bills as a meditation. For many of us, it's one of our least favorite activities, hardly a source of stress reduction! Yet meditation is an intentional activity. Often, stress happens in the background of our lives, nestled within our daily routines. It's no wonder, then, that researchers have found people are more likely to report a positive mood when they are focused on a task, even when the task is "unpleasant." Here's how to turn one of those common daily chores around.

🕐 5 to 10 minutes (You may want to reset the timer multiple times for this meditation.)

1. As you turn your attention toward the activity of paying bills, pause. Check in with yourself and invite a sense of mindfulness for how you're feeling in your body, mood, and state of mind.

2. Remember the attitudes of mindfulness, and ask yourself if any of them might be a good ally for you during this activity. (Attitudes of mindfulness include non-striving, patience, self-trust, acceptance, letting go, nonjudgment, loving-kindness, and beginner's mind; see page 10.) Note your choice before you begin your process.

3. While going about the task, wherever you are and whether you're paying bills online or using pen and ink, keep coming back to your breath. You can think of that breath as home base for your attention.

4. Pause occasionally. When thoughts arise, as with formal meditation, invite attention back to the present. If stressful thoughts arise—for instance, if you're concerned about money—still recognize them as thoughts. You can ask yourself, "Is this happening right now, this very minute?"

(continues)

5. Continue for the entire task. Remember the attitude you identified as support.

6. When finished, congratulate yourself for the time well spent.

7. Note if the practice felt supportive. This can help inspire you to do it again anytime you need to pay bills.

Find Calm within Family Conflict

Stress tests our limits. Even with people we love, sometimes we find ourselves snapping or growing irritable in response to their actions or something they say. Fortunately, there are perspectives we can take to support patience and calm when this occurs. Mindfulness around our feelings and needs supports clarity. As clarity arises, it may add perspective that can steer you toward greater balance, even within a time of conflict.

🕐 10 minutes

1. In your chosen meditation spot, settle in with a comfortable posture that represents dignity and strength.

2. Take time to breathe slowly and regularly with a dedicated focus on the exhale. Bring your mind back when it wanders.

3. Invite the family member with whom you have conflict into your mind. Doing so, note feelings that arise related to the conflict. Honoring how you feel, name them to yourself. Hurt. Anger. Grief. Love. Jealousy.

4. Difficult feelings often reflect an unmet need. Mindfully inquire within, "What do I need right now?" Perhaps there's a need for understanding, a need for honesty. Perhaps there is a need for clarity, or simplicity or freedom.

5. Consider your family member. What do you think they're feeling right now? And what needs might be behind the feelings they have?

6. Continue breathing mindfully, honoring your feelings. Even though we can't control or change what the other person feels or needs, some new clarity may help us relate differently to one another.

7. Finish by placing your hands over your chest, one hand on the other, and just breathing for a while.

Safe Driving in Bad Weather

No one likes to drive in bad weather, but when we don't have a choice, mindfulness can help us be safer drivers and manage stress. Here's a meditation that can prepare you for such a trip in the car. It can help maximize your safety, minimize stress, and perhaps even be enjoyable in some way. Mindfulness is a practice of living all our moments with clarity and ease—even during stressful experiences we'd rather not be having. This meditation is designed to help you become comfortably alert rather than sleepy, so choose your meditation posture while keeping this in mind.

🕐 15 minutes

1. Take some time to be mindful. When you have found a comfortable posture, spend some time with mindful breathing.

2. Breathing slowly and regularly, use each breath to anchor your attention and your sense of being present.

3. Stay with the breath, knowing that this breath can help you regulate your nervous system, which can be a support to you while you're driving.

4. When ready, picture your destination in your mind's eye. Visualize where you are going and picture the route you will take. Keep breathing mindfully.

5. Picture or imagine yourself in the car, driving this route, with the weather conditions at hand. You can even imagine the feelings, thoughts, or physical experience.

6. Imagine arriving safely at your destination and how this will feel.

7. When you are ready, you can conclude the meditation and move on.

8. When you eventually sit down in the driver's seat, reflect on this meditation experience. After you start the car, pause before driving, briefly take some mindful breaths, and picture your route and your safe arrival.

9. You have just prepared yourself to drive mindfully in a way that will help minimize your stress and increase your safety.

Parenting with a Clear and Calm Mind

One of my favorite quotes about mindfulness came from the heart of a meditation retreat, when meditation teacher Christina Feldman defined mindfulness in a beautiful way. She said it is "the willingness and capacity to be present to all our experiences with kindness, curiosity, and discernment." Bringing these qualities into meditation and exploring how they cross over to parenting can be transformative. If you don't have children, this exercise can be applied to any relationship.

🕐 20 minutes (Use a timer.)

1. Give yourself some time for meditation. Find your spot and settle into stillness with mindful breathing. During the meditation, the breath is always here for you as an anchor when your mind drifts off.

2. At some point, distractions will likely arise. The moment you become aware, great!

3. Mindfully investigate what's happening, in mind or body. Are there sounds, sensations, impulses, thoughts, or feelings? Invite an attitude of curiosity.

4. Put out the welcome mat for a mindful attitude you would like to cultivate. Is it patience? Loving-kindness? Beginner's mind? Self-trust? Acceptance or letting be? Letting go? Non-striving?

5. Recall a time when parenting was challenging for you. Imagine applying mindfulness and how that might feel. Try on more scenarios and how you would apply mindfulness in each one.

6. Finish with a period of mindful breathing. If this has been a challenging experience, you might want to place your hands over your heart for a while in the spirit of loving-kindness.

7. When the timer goes off, consider you have just spent time cultivating strengths that have great crossover value for parenting, especially when times get stressful.

End-of-the-Day Regroup

The end of the day is an ideal time to pause, meditate, and reflect. Especially when we're stressed, using this time to come back to ourselves, to allow our bodies to settle and integrate the day's events, positions us to counteract all the stress that may have accumulated during the day or even before. Nothing needs to be done except to let yourself rest and regroup. Tomorrow your mind will be fresh, and you'll have new perspective. Whatever is in motion, whatever is incomplete or unfinished, for right now, it just *is*. This is a time to let things be.

🕐 20 to 30 minutes

1. Find a place to sit quietly or lie down.

2. Take some mindful breaths. As you inhale deeply, feel how the chest expands and the shoulders rise a little. As you exhale, feel the shoulders come down and let the muscles of your chest and all your breathing muscles relax.

3. Breathe mindfully until you start to become aware of the fact that the mind is wandering. That's good to notice! Acknowledge your thoughts, without judgment, and then come back to breathing mindfully.

4. Consider that so many conditions came together that had bearing on the events at hand. Many of them were undoubtedly outside your control. Just breathe as various events from the day come through your mind.

5. As you sift through the events of the day, take your hands and place them on your chest over your heart. Breathe as though breathing into your hands.

6. Continue coming back to the breath, letting go of judgment about the day. Allow it to come to a close. Tomorrow will be a fresh beginning.

7. Come back to body and breath. Let yourself be.

Chronic Stress

We don't always have control over the types of conditions that lead to chronic stress. We do have control over how we respond to them. Mindfulness helps us recognize these opportunities to be in control. In a relatively short amount of time, we can support our body's natural abilities to find balance, calm, and perspective.

Chronic stress often occurs when we have little control or ability to change various factors in our lives. In MBSR classes, however, we often say that as long as you're breathing, there's more right with you than there is wrong. Just because conditions are stressful does not mean that we cannot reclaim our lives and even enjoy them, regardless of what is going on. These meditations can help you build calm, clarity, and perspective into even the most stressful of times.

Mini Meditation

We have the capacity to manage the stress of everyday life. Because each day is different, it can be helpful to build a network of small meditations into your day. Here's how this can work. Choose one mini meditation and link it with a routine behavior for morning, afternoon, and evening. Do it every day so you can make it a habit. To learn more about how to build healthy habits, read *Tiny Habits: The Small Changes That Change Everything* by B. J. Fogg, who developed the evidence-based Tiny Habits method.

🕐 30 seconds to 1 minute

Stress-Relieving Mini Meditations

- Take one to three slow breaths.
- Slowly do a mindful stretch.
- Think of something you're grateful for.
- Take a moment to recall something good that happened today.

Examples of Routine Behaviors

- Waiting for the shower to heat up
- Pouring your morning coffee
- Putting on your seat belt
- After you log on to your computer
- After you come in the door from work
- After lying down in bed at night

Nurturing Calm through Stillness

When our minds are racing, it can feel as though a lot is happening very fast. Mindful attention becomes our ally for finding calm amid the busiest times. Here is an opportunity to stop the world, or at least to recognize that even though the world spins on, where you are standing is stable and supportive. Take some time now to experience this for yourself. We can reclaim time and space for ourselves by noticing the calm and stillness that is already here.

🕐 5 to 45 minutes

1. Find a place to sit that is stable and supportive and where you can be still for a while. Keep your eyes open and your hands resting comfortably in your lap, either palms up or palms down.

2. Find a spot for your gaze on a stable object. If your eyes drift away, bring them back to this fixed spot.

3. Invite your breathing to slow down while you tune in to the stillness of your hands, your body, or anything else in your environment.

4. As you breathe slowly and regularly, notice the reliability of the breath. It's here for you.

5. Allow the gaze to widen to include more of your surroundings, while you continue to breathe slowly and regularly.

6. Tune in to the position of your hands and sensing your hands at rest in this state of non-doing.

7. Think that for right now, nothing else needs to happen.

8. Sense the stillness of your body, right here and right now.

9. Remain with this practice until the timer goes off, just letting yourself be supported by stillness and stability, either within your body or in your environment.

Taking a Break
from Overdrive

Experiencing chronic stress can be like a car getting stuck in overdrive; it's as if there's no "off switch." Similar to a car running on fumes, we eventually run out of gas and become depleted. We need to fill up our tanks. The stress reaction in our bodies wants us to act or react. With this meditation, we will draw on mindful breathing in a specific kind of way. We're going to give our mind something else it can "do" while integrating a built-in rest stage. Giving the mind a chance to take a break can lead to a refreshed outlook with new energy to spare.

🕐 10 to 20 minutes

1. Find both a time and place that give you space to pause and settle in with the breath.

2. Take some deep belly breaths. Breathe all the way down into the bottom of your lungs so that you feel the belly area expand along with the chest.

3. For the exhale, do so through the mouth, but in a passive kind of way where you just let the breath release with no extra effort on your part. Relax your mouth and throat. This active and conscious inhale gives the mind something to do. A specific way of exhaling allows for a release of stress and tension.

4. Continue breathing this way: a deep belly breath as you inhale through the nose, a passive exhale through the mouth with relaxed jaw and throat. You may feel the body start to show signs of relaxation, but if you don't, that's okay.

5. Keep focusing on this two-part breathing for about 10 full breath cycles or so.

6. After the 10 cycles of conscious breathing, just breathe in a way that feels natural to you. Allow 10 to 20 minutes to sit with open awareness. Nothing needs to happen. Just let yourself be.

Priming the Mind
for Happiness

Most moments are safe, but when we are stressed, we are often living as though this is not the case. Our brain and body are always maintaining a degree of protective alertness that leans toward noticing "unpleasant" rather than "pleasant." We can prime our minds to become aware that there are things going on we may enjoy even during times of difficulty. By inclining the mind toward what's "pleasant" rather than what's "unpleasant," we are reclaiming more mental terrain dedicated toward feeling good. It is always there; we are mostly just tuning it out.

🕐 5 to 15 minutes

1. Find a place to sit comfortably with an attitude of relaxed alertness.

2. Choose to be aware.

3. Recall a recent experience of something pleasant or positive that you experienced.

4. As you hold the pleasant experience in mind, investigate it in detail. Notice thoughts, feelings, and sensations that go with it; try to recognize all three categories.

5. As you reflect on the pleasant experience, ask yourself how you are feeling right now. If it is reflecting any aspect of pleasure, acknowledge it.

6. Stay with any feeling of "pleasant" that you notice, allowing it to expand. Really take it in.

7. Stay with this recollection of the positive or pleasant experience for as long as you feel like it, just letting yourself be. Know that you can do this for yourself at any time.

Exploring Sensory Eating

Sensory eating is a valuable way to informally practice meditation because the act of eating is something we all do regularly. Food, however, is an emotional topic for many people. It's something we all tend to enjoy, but we sometimes experience stress related to food as well. There may be dietary concerns, weight or health issues, money stress, or relationship issues that tie in—including loneliness when eating alone. This is a meditation that can help foster a new relationship with food and eating. As with other meditations, we do this for its own sake, but we can also draw on it to explore the sensory nature of eating mindfully, which may be quite pleasant.

🕐 10 to 20 minutes (Timer optional.)

1. At a meal or snack time, before you begin to eat, pause and check in with yourself. Notice how you are feeling physically, mentally, and emotionally. Let go of self-judgment and tune in.

2. Notice whether you are hungry or not, again without judgment.

3. If there is an impulse to begin eating, note how this feels. Check in with your body and sense what an impulse is like on a physical level.

4. Notice thoughts and judgments related to the food.

5. When you are ready, begin eating, mindfully choosing, tasting, chewing, swallowing.

6. Put down your fork between bites and savor what you are choosing.

7. There may be awareness of experiences such as "liking" or "not liking" or "neutral."

8. Eat the rest of your meal mindfully, or until the timer goes off. Before you move on, check in and ask yourself if there is anything you would like to remember from this eating meditation.

The Mindful Shower
or Bath for Chronic Stress

Making this one a regular habit can address chronic stress daily. Most of us have the makings of a spa in our very own homes. Although photos of spas might have images of big fluffy towels, candles, natural wood, and calming music, the basic elements for a restorative shower are generally at our fingertips. Here's how to make your mindful shower or bath a restorative meditation. Hint: The more you can involve your senses, the better. This could include music or nature sounds streamed from your phone to round out the experience.

🕐 10 minutes or more

1. While the water is heating up, do slow, mindful stretches. You're waiting anyway; why not use this for some mindful movement?

2. When getting into the shower, take a few moments to stand and appreciate the transition, especially pleasant sensations, emotions, scents, or visuals. For example, there might be a sigh of relief, standing still for a moment and letting your shoulders relax.

3. Stay connected to yourself as you go about your shower. Notice when the mind wanders away to your 9 a.m. meeting (or wherever), and come back to being fully present in the shower.

4. Whenever you notice something pleasant about the experience, really absorb it. Pause and notice that it feels good. Stay with it.

5. If you're using soap or shampoo, take in the scent, the texture, how it feels to use it on your body or in your hair. Take the time you have and wash mindfully, or just stand under the cascading water and feel the sensations.

6. When ready, finish by standing under the shower, perhaps with eyes closed. Mindfully breathing, allow the world to stop for a moment, just giving yourself this experience of pause and ease.

7. When ready, move forward with your day or evening.

Getting Perspective

42.

Although making healthy life choices can help with long-term stress, it may also be helpful to recognize that we can be at home and find ease wherever we are. When we're stressed, it can seem as if we need to get away from it. That fight-or-flight reaction has a strong "flee" component. Might we be okay wherever we are? This is an activity we often do in MBSR classes. Give yourself a little time to explore this insight-provoking meditation on changing places and perspectives.

🕐 15 minutes

1. In your home, find a place to sit. Choose someplace where you sit on a routine basis.

2. Be aware of where you are. Take some mindful breaths. Notice how you are feeling in your body and any impressions on your thoughts, feelings, or general state of mind. Do so nonjudgmentally.

3. Tune in to your environment and the room around you. Notice things like sound, the objects around you, color, quality of light, view, or anything else.

4. Ask yourself why you are sitting where you are. Do you sit here regularly or for a specific reason?

5. After you spend some time checking in, get up and choose another seat. This time choose one that you don't think you'll like.

6. When you sit down in this new place, go through a similar kind of check-in. How does it feel to sit in this new seat that you thought you would not like? Anything surprising?

7. You can try the same process with other places to sit.

8. Now go back to your original seat.

Mindful Reflection

- How does it feel to be back in your original seat?
- What do you notice now that you've mindfully tried out the other seats?
- Have you learned anything that surprised you?
- What aspect of your experience did not change as you switched seats?
- Maybe you noticed a habitual pattern?
- Perhaps you saw something in your home that you'd never noticed before?
- If you liked or didn't like certain seats, ask yourself why.
- Were you aware of any preconceptions that proved different?
- What would you like to remember from this experience that you can draw on at a different time?

Safe Space Meditation

43.

Although most of our moments are safe, when we are stressed the body is responding as though preparing for the worst. This is natural—it's what has helped us through our evolution as humans to protect ourselves and respond to danger. Now, during this time when our stress reaction may be in overdrive, remember that we are safe and our experience is not just manageable but an opportunity to touch our own wholeness and sense of well-being, regardless of what else is going on.

🕐 15 to 30 minutes

1. Take some time for yourself when you can be undisturbed. Assume a lying position. Look around and get your bearings on the room, the environment around you. Recognize that the environment is basically a safe place right now.

2. Place your hands over your heart, and breathe for a while as though into the hands. Feel the sensations of the breath in the body, bringing the mind back when it wanders. Take some time for your body to become calmer.

3. If you wish, in your mind repeat this phrase or something similar: "May I feel safe and protected from inner and outer harm."

4. Note any symptoms in your body that you relate to as "stress." This would be things such as tension, a racing or pounding heart, shallow breathing, restlessness, and challenging emotions.

5. Note what is on your mind. You may notice worst-case scenario thinking. When worries go to the imagined future, consider that your future self will be better poised to respond then.

6. Most of our moments are safe. Continue breathing as though into your hands, wishing yourself well.

Senses Alive in the Neighborhood

Connecting with our own environment is a reliable break from the interior focus where we start to lose touch with a wider perspective. We can get out of our heads when we take time outside. Look at your neighborhood through mindful eyes, seeing everything as if for the first time. Trying this at different times of day can be delightful. I recently changed my routine to walk during the first morning rays. The flowers are so vibrant at that hour. Dusk may have a calming influence or help you settle at the end of a long day. Whereas slow walking meditation is valuable for periods of formal meditation practice, relatively faster or more normally paced walking outside can be a way to connect to the wider world, with senses alive.

🕐 15 to 40 minutes (Let this be a walking period without music, podcasts, or audiobooks.)

1. Pause before you start your walk to check in with your body.

2. Begin walking. Feel that you are breathing. When you find yourself becoming very active mentally, come back to the breath.

3. As your attention stabilizes on breathing and walking, let awareness expand to feel more, see more, hear more.

4. When something gets your attention, like a vivid flower, a tree, even an interesting crack in the pavement, pause. Allow your visual field to absorb the details of what you are seeing. When ready, resume walking.

5. When sounds get your attention, you can pause and simply listen, curious about what you are hearing.

6. If there are other people around, consider that they, too, experience stress, as well as sensory awareness. We are connected through our common humanity, walking or being present together here and now.

7. Whenever you conclude your walk, pause and check in with how you are feeling now. Is there anything you would like to remember from your experience? Then go on with your day.

Relief from Obsessive Thinking

When we meditate, it's not uncommon for thoughts to take center stage. When stress is chronic, we may find we're ruminating a lot, day and night. Especially when we're stressed, we tend to respond to obsessive thoughts as though they are really happening in this moment. In most instances, this is not the case. This meditation can help you get your bearings when thoughts dominate your attention, especially as they relate to anxiety. It's okay if there's a lot of awareness of thoughts. This meditation is made for exactly that experience.

🕐 20 to 40 minutes

Note: The longer you practice, the more likely the mind has a chance to quiet on its own.

1. Take some time for meditation and start with a focus such as awareness of breathing or mindfulness of sound. As the mind wanders, keep coming back to your chosen focus.

2. When your attention becomes a little more stable, recognize thoughts as if they are a story unfolding.

3. Aim to stay with your primary anchor. There is no need for you to suppress thoughts; just keep recognizing the story when it comes back.

4. Notice components of your thoughts without getting lost in their stories. If thoughts contain imagery, you could note what you're "seeing" in your mind's eye—for instance, "people" or "colors." If you are imagining a conversation or being in a noisy place, you could note "sound" or "talking" or "hearing."

5. Now, picture your thoughts on a movie screen. Imagine that you are sitting in the audience, watching your thought movie unfold. When you start to get drawn in, recognize that you are merely observing the story, you are not in it.

6. Ask yourself if what is happening "on the movie screen" of your mind is true in this very moment; in reality, it's usually not. If that's the case, just recognize it.

7. As needed, come back to your primary anchor while you continue to gain perspective on your thought story.

8. Finish with a simple focus on awareness of breathing or sound. Let yourself be.

The Healing Power
of Awareness

Being mindfully aware can feel like shining a light on whatever is happening right here and now. But the truth is that the light of awareness is always here. When we're mindful, we are tuning in and letting awareness grow. It's like pausing and allowing it to find you. Notice what happens. Because our bodies know how to regulate stress, we may feel our body and mind respond. For instance, if your shoulders are tense, when this experience comes into awareness, we may naturally start to relax them. You can observe how this type of thing occurs and cultivate self-trust during times of stress. We are always in the present moment, where we can respond and care for ourselves. Awareness is the faculty that allows us to do this. Here's how to use the power of awareness itself to ease symptoms of stress through embodied awareness.

🕐 20 minutes

1. Sit or lie down in a relatively quiet place where you have some privacy.

2. Take a deep breath and then exhale, long and slow.

3. Allow the surface supporting you to receive your full weight. Begin to let go of any unneeded effort.

4. When the mind wanders and you recognize that wandering, come back to the immediacy of sound or sensations or anything else.

5. After centering yourself in awareness, just let yourself be.

6. Consciously tune in to any signals from your body that reflect what you think of as "stress."

7. While being aware, make a mindful choice about how to respond to the stress signals coming from your body. Perhaps picture breathing into feelings of tension. You can mindfully stretch and then return to stillness. Or just keep breathing, long and slow, feeling supported. Perhaps something else comes to mind.

8. Recognize that awareness is always already here. Tune in and mindfully respond to what's needed. This might even be welcoming and feeling your emotions.

9. Allow the balance between non-doing and mindful effort to encompass your entire experience.

10. Let yourself be.

The Practice
of Appreciative Joy

When stressed, it's easy to lose touch with being connected to others, whether one-on-one or in the community. We might even feel lonely in a crowded room. Connection to others contributes to our health and resilience to stress. In this meditation, we cultivate connection through "appreciative joy." As with meditations on loving-kindness, this is known as a *cultivation practice*, similar to how we might prepare a garden. We cultivate the right conditions for empathetic joy to arise on its own, so it can blossom in its own time.

🕐 20 minutes

1. Find a place to sit in meditation for a while and spend some time with mindful breathing.

2. Picture in your mind someone dear to you. It might even be a pet.

3. Picture how they are when happy, even joyful. Imagine the details of their face and posture. Get a sense of how their bodies express this happiness.

4. As you hold them in awareness, think "May your happiness continue to grow, may your sources of joy multiply." Imagine you're breathing in this sentiment and exhaling any pain or loneliness, whatever is here.

5. Now, hold yourself in mind. "May my happiness continue to grow, may my sources of joy multiply." Imagine you're breathing in this sentiment and exhaling any pain or loneliness, whatever is here.

6. Next, hold in mind all beings, thinking "May our happiness continue to grow and sources of joy multiply." Again, imagine you're breathing in this sentiment and exhaling any pain or loneliness, whatever is here. Let it go.

7. You don't have to feel anything, but put out the welcome mat for these wishes to grow. You may not immediately feel the sympathetic joy, yet if you act as if you do, this allowing creates space for it to arise on its own.

8. After repeating the phrases for a while, sit with how you feel inside. There's no right way to feel. Just let yourself be.

Releasing Worry
and Finding Peace

Worry is one of the symptoms of stress, and it often happens unconsciously. Whether we're aware of it or not, when our mind reflects fear and concern, it's often making assumptions about how things are going to turn out, or the worst-case scenario. Helping to tone down worries with perspective goes a long way to reducing the impact of stress. With this meditation, we're going to practice in a way that helps us release worry and find peace.

🕐 20 minutes

1. Find your meditation spot and take a posture that supports a state of relaxed alertness.

2. Gather attention and bring it to rest on the breath. You can start with some deeper, fuller breaths and then settle in with breathing in such a way that takes the least amount of effort.

3. When worries arise in your mind, acknowledge these worried thoughts. They are just thoughts. You can even simply note "worrying." Keep coming back to the body and breath.

4. When worry arises, mindfully ask yourself this question and note your inner response: "Am I making any assumptions right now?" Note the answer and come back to the breath and body.

5. Continue meditating with this constellation of experiences—breath, body, mental experience—noting assumptions for 15 minutes or so.

6. As you move forward into your day or night, bring the spirit of this meditation with you. When worries arise, continue to ask yourself, "Am I making any assumptions right now?"

Befriending the Self-Critic

A reflection of stress is self-criticism. Especially when there's a lack of control, the part of us that wants control will turn toward self-blame. This toxic inner experience leads to more tension and stress. It can affect every aspect of our lives, including our self-esteem, self-confidence, and feelings of worthiness. It's not uncommon to treat other people better than we treat ourselves, especially when we are being self-critical. Recall the kind of attitude that you might extend to a good friend when they are stressed or struggling. Patience? Forgiveness? Tolerance? Kindness? Whatever comes to mind, offer this same mental attitude toward yourself.

🕐 30 minutes (Use a timer.)

1. Take some time for yourself and a period of meditation practice. In this practice, meet yourself as you might a dear friend. Consider the attitude you might invite in.

2. While maintaining a focus on your breath, let awareness also include awareness of your body. There's no need to make anything happen. Recognize how you're feeling, self-critical thoughts, and anything else that comes into awareness.

3. Picture in your mind a friend who is down on themselves. How might you respond?

4. There is no experience that can't be met with perspective and kindness. How might you convey loving acceptance to a friend? Offer this to yourself.

5. Continue meditating, meeting any part of your experience as you might a good friend.

6. When the timer goes off, take a deep breath and check in. Ask yourself if you'd like to remember anything from this meditation to draw upon at a future time.

Examining Chronic Pain

Our inner conditions are constantly changing. Recognizing this may help us begin to relate to the passing nature of all the elements of our experiences, including pain. All sensations, feelings, thoughts, impulses—these are all temporary. With mindfulness, we hold our experience, without judgment or analyzing, to the best of our abilities. It's better not to do this meditation when you are feeling at your worst. Meditate at a time when your pain feels relatively manageable.

🕐 30 minutes (Use a timer.)

1. Find some time for yourself, day or night. Lie or sit down.

2. Give your mind a relatively neutral place to rest with mindfulness of the breath.

3. When pain comes into awareness, let go of calling the sensations "pain" and instead investigate its qualities. Especially recognize if it changes, and keep paying attention as this happens. Are the sensations sharp, dull, pulsing, or radiating, or something else? Is there pressure, tingling, burning, heat, or coolness? Note other qualities like deep or shallow, still or moving, large or small.

4. Keep coming back to the breath if you start to get lost.

5. When emotions arise—be they fear, dread, self-blame—recognize your feelings, because they are already here. They come and go.

6. When thoughts come into awareness, note qualities like assumptions, planning, remembering.

7. Keep coming back to the breath for stability of attention.

8. Invite an attitude of loving-kindness into your body by asking yourself, "Where's kindness here?"

9. If there's a desire to stop the meditation early, make a deal with yourself to stay for at least another six seconds. Things may change.

10. When the timer goes off, spend a few moments just breathing and letting yourself be.

Emotional Stress

Mindfulness is a form of wise attention that can help us reconnect with a sense of our wholeness, while also honoring the broad range of emotions that may get stirred up by a stressful time. Meditation can help us recognize the temporary nature of feelings, how no feeling is final or a permanent condition. By responding consciously to our feelings, we can access their wisdom, get in touch with our own needs, and become increasingly resilient through the power of awareness.

Ease Anxiety

Anxiety can mean different things to different people. Consider this when you name something "my anxiety." For the purpose of this meditation, see if you can let go of the term and focus on elements of your direct experience. Since stress symptoms related to anxiety can be disorienting and even chaotic, we will also aim to simplify your experience. The benefits of this meditation are cumulative. The more you do it, the more likely you will gain confidence in your ability to self-regulate around the symptoms of stress. This meditation is short by design, so that it is accessible regardless of the intensity of your anxiety.

🕐 30 seconds to 5 minutes

1. At any point that you recognize you are feeling anxiety, pause—whether the middle of the night or in a grocery store aisle. Consciously come to a stop.

2. Focus attention specifically on the breath flowing into and out of your nose. We're making our focal point as clear and simple as possible.

3. Breathe slowly and regularly.

4. When distractions arise (they likely will), let them be.

5. To the best of your ability (not perfectly), keep inviting awareness of breathing to the foreground while distractions remain in the background.

6. If you start analyzing the anxiety, come back to awareness of your breath. Keep it simple.

7. Keep breathing mindfully while your body gradually becomes calmer. Watch for signs like your mind becoming clearer, your heart rate slowing, and emotions becoming more even.

8. It's normal for anxiety to come and go as we learn how to self-regulate with mindfulness. Be patient and come back to this meditation as often as you wish.

9. When you finish meditating, consider that you'll be taking the breath with you. You can breathe mindfully anywhere you go.

Sleep Serenely

Most of us have an occasional night of disrupted sleep. With insomnia, we may even feel like we are broken and have lost the ability to sleep. Thoughts do not cause insomnia. They are just in your awareness more because you're hyperalert. Mindfulness can help us gain perspective on what is happening, so that our bodies can relax and let sleep come. You'll be catching that sleep wave before you know it and restoring your faith in your body's ability to sleep.

🕐 1 to 30 minutes

1. When you realize that you are awake and sleep is not coming easily, turn to mindfulness practice.

2. Gather your attention and bring it to focus gently on the breath. Doing this, you may recognize how strongly thoughts are pulling you into alertness.

3. Anchor your attention on the breath, or bring attention to feelings and sensations in your feet.

4. Keep bringing attention back to the breath or to sensations in your feet.

5. If you become aware of what's on your mind, consider that at this hour, your mind is likely not capable of making decisions or choices about future actions or events. Save it for tomorrow.

6. Keep bringing attention back to the breath or to sensations in your feet.

7. If desired, place a hand over your heart and imagine breathing in kindness, or say a comforting phrase to yourself.

8. Forget about ideas of sleep and let rest be your priority. Feel yourself ease into resting.

Put an End to Panic

Panic can be soothed by learning how not to react to the reaction. There is no need to think your way out of the panic reaction. Even though panic can feel intense and scary, it will run its course and subside on its own. We can learn to trust the body and get better at staying calm. No matter where you are, whether in a store aisle, in bed in the middle of the night—wherever—mindfulness can support the body and mind, restoring balance. You can help your body unlearn the pattern of panic attacks.

🕐 1 to 5 minutes

1. When you recognize that the mind is ramping up and you're starting to experience panic symptoms, breathe in this specific way: inhale through the nostrils, exhale through the mouth with pursed lips (as though blowing out a candle).

2. Continue breathing long and slow with awareness of breath in your nose, exhaling through pursed lips.

3. Continue with the mindful breathing; anxious thoughts can stay in the background. No need to make them go away.

4. As you continue to do this, your body will calm down. The more you do this meditation, the faster it will resolve.

5. When ready, move on with your day or night.

Confidence Booster

Mindfulness encompasses what is now termed the "mind-body connection." There is a feedback loop with information going between body and mind, where each relies on the other to stay in alignment. This is confirmed with research, such as that by psychologist and author Amy Cuddy, which reveals how confidence increases or decreases relative to body posture. We can draw upon the findings to benefit our own confidence whenever needed.

🕐 1 to 2 minutes (A timer is helpful but not necessary.)

1. Take some time to pause and give yourself mindful attention.

2. Stand upright, in mountain pose (see page 44). Balance evenly over both feet.

3. Check in with your body and notice how you are feeling right now. You can even notice your posture and see if it reflects your mood in some way.

4. Now assume a posture in which you take up more space physically. This could be reaching arms overhead or out to the side. (Think Superman or Wonder Woman.) The more space you take up, the more it's seen to demonstrate dominant behavior.

5. Hold this posture for a minute.

6. When the timer goes off, check in with yourself again and notice your energy level, your mood, how your body feels, or anything else.

Self-Comfort Remedy

Some of us respond to stress with comfort behaviors that don't serve us in the long run. This is called "maladaptive coping." One of these is stress eating, but some other common ones are binge-watching TV, overworking, drinking too much alcohol, and other avoidant behaviors that ultimately don't help our stress. Mindfulness can help us recognize habitual patterns so we can change them and live healthier lives. This mindfulness practice has cumulative benefits.

🕐 1 to 5 minutes

1. When you become aware of an impulse to use an unhealthy coping strategy, pause and take a few minutes for this practice.

2. Wherever you are, standing or sitting, eyes open or closed, turn your attention inward.

3. Check in: How are you feeling physically? Are there any symptoms related to stress?

4. What is on your mind, or was on your mind earlier in the day?

5. What is your mental state? Are you bored? Restless? Wanting to distract yourself?

6. What are you feeling? There may be layers of emotions, or you may feel emotionally numb.

7. What are you really needing?

8. Bring mindfulness to the feeling of discomfort that comes with this impulse. I heard meditation teacher Noah Levine refer to it as "sitting with the ouch." Just like an annoying itch, if we don't give it attention, often within six seconds or so, the impulse will pass.

9. Take three long, deep breaths. While "sitting with the ouch" is uncomfortable, it's not a terminal condition. Enjoy the mindful breaths while waiting for it to pass—and it will.

10. Congratulate yourself. With practice, new healthy behaviors will grow stronger and stronger.

Settle Your Nerves with 4-7-8 Breathing

At times we may find we are nervous or jittery. This could reflect anxiety, being overstimulated by current events, or anything else that revs you up. There is a lot you can do to assist with this, and a classic meditation used to bring remarkable calm is called 4-7-8 breathing. It is said to help balance the nervous system so that "fight or flight" can become "rest and calm."

🕐 5 minutes (Timer optional.)

1. Take some time to pause for a few minutes so you can give your attention fully to the practice.

2. Gather attention and bring it to mindfully settle on the breath.

3. Breathe in for a count of 4.

4. Hold the breath for a count of 7.

5. Exhale to a count of 8.

6. Repeat 3 to 10 cycles (whatever amount you would like, or until the timer goes off).

Confrontation Confidence

Confronting someone or a group can be scary. Mindful communication can be a resource to help bring perspective, clarity, and compassion to the experience. We don't have control over other people's reactions, but we do have control over our attitude and our words. This can involve consideration of our overall intention. Keep in mind that life rarely follows the script we have for it. Stay open to any outcome.

🕐 5 to 10 minutes

1. When you become aware that there is an emotional charge to a communication interchange, pause and check in with yourself. Wherever you are, pause, check in. Notice what you are feeling, how your body may be reflecting any symptoms of stress, your state of mind, what you are feeling.

2. Get clear:

   - What do you need from the confrontation? How will you know your need was met?
   - What are your intentions?
   - Is what you have to say helpful in some way?
   - Is this a good time for you to do this?

3. Picture the interchange. Envision yourself staying with your feelings and needs and your desired outcome.

4. When the timer goes off, know that you are more prepared to communicate effectively and care for yourself during any confrontation.

Clear Decision-Making

Decisions can be hard sometimes, especially when we don't have a clear picture of what the future will bring. How can we be here for ourselves, flexible to changing conditions, while also steering our lives in the direction of our dreams and goals? Although we don't have complete control over life, we do have the ability to become clearer about what we want. Here is a meditation for clarity.

🕐 10 to 20 minutes

1. Take some time for mindfulness practice. Find a place to sit, take a mindful posture, and breathe in a way that is focused and intentional.

2. Breathing regularly on the in and out, allow yourself to settle for a while. When you allow space for it, this will occur in its own time.

3. When you have gained some degree of concentration, mindfully ask yourself, "What do I really want?" Listen inwardly for the answer.

4. After some time, ask again, this time, "What do I really, really want?" Wait for the answer to bubble up from within you. Sitting and breathing, be patient with this process. When the answer arises, sit with it for a while.

5. Pose the question one last time: "What do I really, really, *really* want?" This takes some deep inner listening, and it may take a while. Sit and breathe with the question in the meantime.

6. When the answer arises, just sit with it.

7. Let yourself be, honoring this inner clarity. Being clear about what you desire allows you to move in the direction of your dreams and goals.

Many Waves, One Ocean

When we're depressed, it's not uncommon to feel detached or disconnected from ourselves, others, even our own bodies. There may also be symptoms like anxiety and feeling caught in rumination, where thoughts we have already experienced a thousand times keep running through our minds as if they were new and scary. Mindfulness meditation can help restore a sense of connection to the broader whole in ourselves, others, and the world at large. Scientific research has demonstrated that the brains of meditators are different, reflecting a greater sense of connection.

🕐 20 minutes

1. Take a lying-down position, on your back, with arms alongside your body and your feet hip distance apart.

2. Consciously let the surface you're on take your full weight so that it's possible to let go. Don't make any extra effort to lie down; the ground is supporting you.

3. Invite awareness to the rhythm of the breath in your body, just noticing that you're breathing.

4. Picture the in breath like a wave rolling in and onto a beach. With the exhale, think of it flowing back out, becoming ocean again.

5. Just keep breathing, picturing the wave. The kind of wave doesn't matter, whether a tiny wave or a huge, crashing wave. No need to control the breath.

6. Mindful awareness is the ocean. The wave is never truly separate from the ocean, even if it seems separate at times. Even coming ashore, the wave is still ocean.

7. Think of all the other waves in the ocean. Not just your breath waves, but the waves of common humanity. So many waves. A Zen quote reflects that when the wave becomes aware that it is ocean, it becomes enlightened.

8. As you breathe, with as little effort as possible, just let yourself be.

Healing Grief

Just as the ocean has its waves, everyone's life has its own flow—ups and downs, coming and going. One of the most painful emotions, grief, is not really a single feeling; it has layers. Here's an example: An aspect of grief I recall during my divorce involved anxiety that I would lose a connection with my in-laws, who had become family to me. As I brought mindful inquiry to the layers, I was surprised that beneath these painful emotions was love. Being present to grief through mindfulness requires patience and tenderness. Give yourself some space for healing with this simple meditation.

🕐 20 to 30 minutes

1. Find a time for some mindfulness meditation when your grief is not at its most intense. Take the position of your choosing, and let your attention settle on the breath.

2. When your attention on the breath becomes relatively stable, turn the focus to open monitoring. This is simply open awareness of whatever is arising. You can return to the breath whenever needed to stabilize your focus, especially if strong feelings arise.

3. Whatever feelings arise, let them be. Note them as simply as you can.

4. As you investigate the feelings, notice how they may be changing. Perhaps alternating or maybe jumping around. At times perhaps they merge together.

5. If big waves of emotions come, give them space. Focusing on the breath can help with staying connected.

6. Just as you notice the waves of emotions, also notice when they subside. You can feel into this as well. What does it feel like when a wave subsides?

7. Consider placing your hands over your heart or on your abdomen, and breathe as though breathing into your hands. Alternatively, give yourself a hug.

8. Let go of having any specific kind of experience, and let yourself be.

A New Lens for Public Speaking

Fear of public speaking is one of the most common human fears. Many would rather do almost anything else. Here is a meditation to help you prepare for public speaking and approach the actual experience when anxiety arises. Mindfulness can help reframe the experience of anxiety as something like excitement (the body experience is quite similar). Mindfulness is being present to our experiences without trying to change them, but we can also use mindful inquiry to investigate an experience like anxiety. The way we interpret an experience can make all the difference. This technique can go a long way to reducing the impact of stress related to public speaking and other anxiety-provoking events.

🕐 20 minutes (Use a timer or do this spontaneously.)

1. Before the event, take some time to meditate and calm the mind and body.

2. While breathing with awareness, picture the event in detail: the environment, the audience, how your body might be positioned.

3. Envision the type of experience you'll have. Imagine all the things you might feel. Perhaps a pounding heart, racing mind, or sweaty palms? These are common to all types of stress.

4. To be here for yourself with mindfulness, recognize that your interpretations are optional. If yours is "I'm terrified!" consider it as "I'm beyond myself with excitement to present this information!"

5. Your audience will be happy to experience your excitement. You don't have to hide it.

6. Picture yourself enjoying the people in the room. Take the focus off yourself and think of how unique they all are.

7. Let go of assumptions that you know how things will turn out.

8. Spend some more time with mindful breathing until the timer goes off.

62.

Transforming Jealousy

Jealousy can be one of the most painful and frustrating experiences in life. It's almost impossible to talk ourselves out of certain emotional and mental states. Feelings of jealousy can hang on or come back again and again. There is often an added layer of feeling bad about ourselves for being jealous, which can then intensify the experience. Here's a meditation to help loosen the grip of the toxic-feeling emotion.

🕐 20 minutes

1. Establish your meditation posture and spend time with either awareness of breath or open monitoring of awareness.

2. Place your hands over your heart and breathe for a while.

3. Feel your heart beating and your lungs breathing. Stay with this experience as you allow your concentration to deepen.

4. When ready, recall the person who is the object of your jealousy. Holding them in mind, say to yourself:

    Just like me, this person has a heart that beats and lungs that breathe.

    Just like me, this person wants to feel safe and be free from harm.

    Just like me, this person wants to be happy and peaceful and live with ease and kindness.

5. Continue breathing with your hands over your heart. There's no need to feel a special way. Just let yourself be. Over time you may be pleasantly surprised about what this meditation yields.

Cool Down Anger

Anger can be one of the most challenging feelings and something most of us would prefer not to feel. It is also a natural emotion and one that will run its course in due time. If it arises in meditation, we can witness it and recognize that, in the moment, there's nothing we need to do about it. Just let it be. When we are intensely angry, reason and logic can be suppressed. Meditation is an opportunity to be here for ourselves while our nervous system can gain perspective and clarity. We can learn what essentially fuels our angry reactions and what helps us find our footing again.

🕐 20 to 30 minutes (Use a timer.)

1. Take some time for meditation. Set a timer and find a meditation posture that works for you in the place where you are.

2. Start with awareness of breath, connecting with your body and mind. If there are strong feelings like anger present, recognize they are there without trying to change them.

3. Stay with mindful breathing for about five minutes, then switch the focus to awareness of the whole body, perhaps doing a body scan (see page 36).

4. Often with strong emotional reactions, the mind becomes swept into thinking very easily. Before we know it, we're in a river of feelings, being carried downstream.

5. Engage curiosity about what is happening in *this* moment. Bring attention back to the present.

6. The body will often mirror the mind in some way. Spend some time with body awareness as the anchor for your attention.

7. Invite awareness to be inclusive of sound, and listen mindfully. As the mind moves into thoughts and feelings, come back to sound as a resting place.

(continues)

8. Invite loving-kindness for the fact that you're being challenged by the strong emotions or accompanying thoughts. Breathe in compassion for your suffering; breathe out, mentally releasing the intensity. Stay with the loving-kindness breathing for about five minutes.

9. When the timer goes off, take a moment to check in with yourself and ask if there's anything you would like to remember for a future time.

Help for Regret

All our experiences and actions are a culmination of what came before them. Some are within our control, some are not. In this meditation, you can consider the countless conditions, personal and impersonal, that led to the experience of regret. Healing can occur when we reclaim a sense of our basic goodness and our humanity among whatever we regret. This same meditation applies to any feelings of guilt or shame that we may possess.

🕐 20 to 30 minutes (Use a timer.)

1. Take a little time and space for practice when you can allow yourself room for all your feelings, whatever they may be.

2. Find the breath and let it be an anchor for the mind. When the mind drifts, come back to awareness of the breath.

3. As your attention stabilizes, call to mind the regret you're holding.

4. Through mindful inquiry, consider all the events, recent or from the very distant past, that may have led to the regret.

5. Consider the countless thoughts, impulses, and conditioning along the way that also contributed. Include yours as well as those of others.

6. Going back even generations, consider all the people, known or unknown, who may have contributed to the eventual regret.

7. While inviting self-compassion, as you inhale, think of breathing in the pain or suffering that has resulted in the feelings of regret, your own or that of others. Imagine that whatever goodness is within you is transforming it into something that serves you. As you breathe it out, imagine this energy of basic goodness transforming the regret into self-kindness.

8. Until the timer goes off, continue breathing this way, tapping into this source of basic goodness within you, letting it permeate the pain and suffering.

65. Honoring All Emotions

Honoring our emotions can help us manage stress as we also recognize that our feelings do not define us. All emotions are temporary, but sometimes we overidentify with certain feelings, blocking out others. We might think things like "I was angry all day." Anger might have been one aspect of your day. But if you examine it, there may have also been many moments of stillness, serenity, and calm.

🕐 30 minutes (Use a timer.)

1. Find your meditation spot and bring attention to the breath.

2. When your focus gets stronger, include your body sensations as part of the focus.

3. As you note awareness of thoughts or feelings, stay anchored to your breath and body sensations.

4. When you get caught in the story line, come back to the present.

5. Mindfully investigate your experience of emotions.

6. Be willing to drop a thought or feeling. Just recognizing it is enough, be it sadness, anger, fear, happiness, or whatever emotion you are experiencing.

7. Sometimes we fall in the river of emotions and don't realize it until we're quite a way downstream. As soon as you recognize being lost in the stream, you have become mindful. It's as though you're now standing on the bank where your footing is sure. Let yourself be.

8. Continue this practice until the timer goes off. Then ask yourself if there's anything you'd like to remember for a future time.

Big Life Events

Mindfulness meditation is not a one-size-fits-all practice but one that is adaptable. It is spacious, flexible, and caring. During times of great change, it can help us gain perspective to see the big picture. We can draw from a variety of ways to practice mindfulness that help us stay centered, remain stabilized, and foster resilience, even when experiencing the kind of rapid change that often accompanies big life events.

For everyone, even the most experienced meditator, big life events may come along that throw us off our game. Mindful ways of coping are not always clear to us, especially if we're experiencing certain types of stress for the first time. These meditations offer support and perspective for how to bring mindfulness to some of the most challenging circumstances life can present.

Mindfulness
after Job Loss

The loss of a job brings change on numerous levels. In addition to the emotional reaction, there is often an adjustment to an abrupt change in schedule. Keeping any degree of regularity can be a great support, as can developing small moments of mindfulness throughout the day. The Tiny Habits method, demonstrated here, is one that builds on the stability of routine behavior, creating new healthy behaviors. It's possible to develop lasting healthy habits that support the regulation of stress reactions that may occur during this time of rapid change between jobs.

🕐 Daily, connected with one to three routine behaviors, for up to 30 seconds (Shorter is better when it comes to Tiny Habits.)

1. Identify between one and three routine things you do every day, no matter what. These might include making a cup of coffee, coming home from shopping, or walking the dog.

2. After each routine, connect this tiny meditation: Pause and take one to three long, slow breaths. Then move on with your day. Do this each time you complete your chosen routine behavior.

3. Do this daily. It won't take long before it becomes a habit. These small mindful pauses will support your resilience as you make your way through this stressful time.

Five-Minute
Island of Calm

Although big life events can feel destabilizing, it's always possible to find some stillness and calm. The image of an island can be a nice one for meditation, because spending time within a buffer of solitude can be restorative. It doesn't have to be long—five minutes can be enough. Try giving yourself this gift.

🕐 5 minutes (Timer optional.)

1. Take some time for some stillness. Sit on the floor for added stability.

2. Find the breath; breathe slowly and regularly for a few breath cycles. Then breathe naturally.

3. Find balance within the sitting posture, with your weight centered evenly over your hips and your head centered between your shoulders.

4. Feel the support of the floor. Even the support of our environment can help provide stability in knowing what is here for us.

5. Recognize the boundaries of your body, surrounded by space, with the breath at your center, sitting in stillness. Consider this island of personal space is here for you.

6. Notice the space around your body, a 365-degree kind of awareness. Recognize the space behind you, to the front and the sides, above and below. While the world goes on, this place of calm is here for you.

7. Stay with open monitoring (sometimes referred to as "just sitting") and breath awareness until the timer goes off.

Becoming a Parent

One of the most transformative life events can be having a baby or adopting a child. In the process, our relationship to our own identity goes through a process of change. While parenting a baby or adopting even an older child, we may need to adjust our expectations for the time we can give to meditation. For instance, rather than 30 minutes of sitting quietly by yourself, meditation for busy parents might be numerous 30-second intervals. Just a few seconds can help you re-center and find yourself amid all your responsibilities of caring for a little one. Here's how to practice.

🕐 30 seconds to several minutes

1. Starting in the morning, as you become aware that you are awake, stay in bed for some mindful breathing. Adopt an intentional posture, placing your hands over your heart. Breathe mindfully for several cycles before moving on with your day.

2. Transition intervals, however unpredictable as they may be, do occur during the day. For instance, after you pick up your child, spend some time with mindful breathing. This can be a time of connecting, with both your child and yourself. Breathe mindfully for a few breath cycles, while standing in place. An older child can breathe along with you.

3. While washing dishes, bring mindfulness to the sensations of warm water and the repetitive movements of washing, drying, or placing items in the dishwasher. Breathe mindfully.

4. During times when you recognize that you are alone—however rare—consciously pause. You can be standing, sitting, or lying down. You can be in the bathroom, in the car, or somewhere else. Place your hands over your heart or abdomen and breathe mindfully.

5. When you go to bed or lie down, before you drift off, think of one thing you are grateful for.

Healing a
Violation of Self

The stress caused by a traumatic event, such as theft or assault, can be utterly disorienting. There's a level of personal violation, but there may also be confusion, strong emotions, and rumination about the event. Recovery is a process that takes its own time, and you may consider the help of a therapist for support. The truth is, most moments are safe, and mindfulness can help us return to feelings of security.

🕐 5 to 20 minutes (Use a timer.)

1. Take time for yourself. Consciously note that this is time just for you, away from your responsibilities.

2. Stabilize your attention, either through focused breathing or just sitting with awareness.

3. Recognize any feelings present. If there are no specific feelings present, look for clues in bodily tension, restlessness, or ease.

4. Breathing into any tension, as you exhale, think, "Safety is here for me, and I am safe in this moment." While staying with your breath, picture or recall all the ways you can think of that signify this.

5. When your mind starts to go into stressful thoughts, come back to what can be noted of your present experience, wherever you are. Keep breathing.

6. Invite your body to relax further with each exhale, thinking, "Safety is here for me, and I am safe in this moment."

7. Keep coming back to what can be sensed of the present, no matter where your mind drifts, thinking, "Safety is here for me, and I am safe in this moment."

8. Stay with the practice until the timer goes off. Then place your hands over your heart and breathe as if into your hands. Consider that this practice is always here for you, day or night.

Mending the Heart

There's nothing that shatters the heart like a breakup, a point in time when everything that comes next is like a free fall. Familiar benchmarks related to the rhythms and routines of being part of a couple are no longer there as a reference point. In these moments, it's easy to become disoriented. Many kinds of feelings arise. You can draw on the "Emotional Stress" section for support with grief, anger, sadness, and other challenging feelings. Here, we'll focus on a meditation to garner strength and resilience amid the new normal.

🕐 10 to 30 minutes (Use a timer.)

1. Give yourself some time for simplicity, in a neutral place that does not remind you of your relationship.

2. Find a stable sitting posture that represents a kind of dignity and stability, regardless of how you feel emotionally.

3. Stabilize attention, either through mindful awareness of breath or open monitoring, "just sitting" with awareness.

4. Become mindful of thoughts that come and go. Whatever the content, be willing to drop a thought. Many are probably thoughts you have had many times previously. If you wish, you can note, "Not right now."

5. If your logical self wants a reason for doing this, consider that each time you drop a thought, you're helping your heart-mind become more resilient. You can support this process of strength and freedom, building resilience consciously along the way.

6. Continue noting thoughts and building this integration and new resilience. When the timer goes off, regardless of how you feel, know that you have done a great service to your own healing. Later in the day or week, you may see signs of this.

Embracing Vacation

Although one might think of vacation as the opposite of stressful, the truth is that many find it challenging to relax right away. It's not uncommon for thoughts about work to linger, not to mention the amount of preparation that usually goes into planning a trip. Even a staycation can have stressors. Here's how to get the most out of your vacation time. Consider doing this before your vacation begins, and continue it into the first day or two.

🕐 10 minutes

1. Take some time for yourself away from responsibilities. Spend some time with mindful breathing or open monitoring practice.

2. Check in with how your body is feeling. Get an internal weather report. What is your mood like? Overcast? Sunny and warm? Cloudy with a chance of rain? Connect with your body and read your energy level.

3. When thoughts arise, bring them back to the breath or open monitoring, recognizing what's happening in the present. You'll start to have a sense of what is on your mind.

4. Be willing to drop a thought. Each time you drop a thought is like clearing items off your desk.

5. Trust in the process of mental sorting that's happening in the background while keeping your breath in the foreground.

6. Let yourself be.

Wedding Bliss

Change brings stress. Even happy or joyous occasions can be stressful because of how the body and mind respond to the added pressures and complex events that occur. Marriage is a process, it's not a singular event. Even on the day of marriage, there are many parts and aspects. On the days leading up to the wedding, there are various things that transpire on a practical level. There is also the complexity of our relationships. Here's a meditation to help you find equanimity during this time of rapid change.

🕐 15 minutes

1. Find some time for yourself during your day. If privacy is an issue, this might mean taking some time alone in the car, in your bathroom, or on a walk. But find a quiet and private place for you.

2. Start by just coming to stillness and letting yourself be. Let go of the "doing" mode. Let go of planning, rehearsing, or any other thoughts you may have.

3. You can focus on breath awareness, but even that may feel like a lot of effort right now. This may be a time when the meditation practice of open monitoring, just sitting with awareness and letting yourself be, can be of great value.

4. Allow your mindfulness to expand to include awareness of whatever is arising. Very simply, we might call this just sitting with awareness. Mindfulness can hold whatever is arising, including what is on your mind and awareness of sensations, sounds, environment, and any distractions.

5. When your mind starts to go into planning or rehearsing types of thoughts, just come back to what can be noted of your present experience, wherever you are.

6. When the timer goes off, bring mindfulness to one to three breath cycles, and then move on with your day.

Loss of a Loved One

Nothing compares with the experience of losing a loved one. When it comes to stress, there is understandably both acute and chronic stress. The amount of change we experience is huge, regardless of the type of relationship one had, or whether the death was a surprise or the end of a long illness. The loss is a life adjustment, both psychologically and environmentally. Here is a meditation to help you find equanimity amid some changes that occur, both short-term and long-term.

🕐 15 minutes (Use a timer.)

1. Invite calm by breathing slowly and regularly. If strong emotions arise at any point, it's okay to pause the meditation and just let them flow. This can be like riding the rapids of a river. Eventually, however long, they will subside.

2. Place your hands on your abdomen, right under your ribcage, and breathe in so that you can feel your hands moving outward with the inhale and then settle again with the exhale.

3. As you make space for the breath with the inhale, consider that you are making space also for any feelings, thoughts, or other distractions. It can all be held by the meditation practice.

4. With each exhale, invite your body to relax. It's okay to still feel tension or jumbled thoughts or feelings.

5. When the timer goes off, check in with your body and mind. Ask yourself if there is anything you'd like to remember for a future time.

Preparing for a Move

Facing a move, whether to a new home in the same town or one many miles away, is not a single moment but countless moments. This is where a perspective on mindfulness as being not just a singular focus of attention, but rather a way of being, is helpful. With a move, the practice is bringing perspective to the process in order to maximize resilience and manage stress. Mindfulness is not about some steady tranquil state; it's being able to approach each moment with intentional awareness and the attitudes of mindfulness (see page 10).

🕐 20 minutes

1. Find some time in the morning or at the end of the day for quiet and privacy.

2. Stabilize your focus by breathing regularly on the in and out breaths.

3. Consider the day you have ahead.

4. Picture what you expect of the day. As you go through the sequence of events, picture yourself being mindful as you proceed through the day. For example, while packing boxes, there might be slowing down and doing so mindfully. Check in with how your body might feel as you go through each motion.

5. You can even imagine the types of moods or emotions that might occur. If you think you'll become irritable at some point, as we might when under stress, envision how you may mindfully respond to irritation.

6. Picture going through the entire day with mindfulness. The day may or may not unfold exactly as planned (things usually don't), but you have now primed your mind to draw on mindfulness throughout.

7. Stay with the visualization of the mindful day until the timer goes off.

Self-Trust through Divorce

Like marriage, divorce is not a singular event. At any point, however, stress is likely part of it. Whatever emotions arise, they are unique to you in this very moment. They are also ever-changing. One quality of mindfulness that may assist with the entire process of divorce is the development of self-trust. This will be fuel for resilience now and continue long beyond the process of divorce. Trust that you will find your way.

🕐 20 minutes

1. Find for yourself some quiet time during the day, some time just for you.

2. Spend some time simply noticing whatever arises in awareness. This could be what is on your mind, or consciousness of sensations, sounds, environment, or distractions.

3. Sense the support of the surface that you're sitting upon. Invite the big and small muscles of your body to relax, and let your body be heavy, supported by gravity.

4. The mind goes out, taking in perceptions of many things, and then comes back to awareness of body, mind, or emotions. Recognize your own center.

5. Awareness is always occurring. Note this ability to tune in consciously, to connect moment to moment. Trust that you can find your way.

6. Attention goes outward, then it touches back in. You can come back to yourself, again and again. Note this ability to come back. Through the entire process that is divorce, you can come back to yourself again and again, however events unfold.

7. Stay with this meditation until the timer goes off.

76. Balance in Times of Change

During big life events, it's natural to be thrown off balance. A movement practice with a focus on finding balance can be a great support. Trust that you can find your way back into balance, no matter what throws you off. Your body can help you find your way. Since challenging our balance requires concentration, this is also a great meditation to help settle down a racing mind.

🕐 20 minutes

1. Find enough space to stand and bring your arms out to your sides.

2. Stand upright with your weight evenly balanced over both feet. This is called mountain pose.

3. Do this slowly, as a meditation. Bring your mind back when it wanders. Shift your weight from side to side, from foot to foot. Lean forward and backward slightly, just enough to feel slightly off balance. Then come back to center.

4. Bring the arms out to your sides, parallel to the ground.

5. Continue moving slowly and mindfully, and shift your weight onto your right foot, using the arms to help you balance.

6. When ready, bring the right foot back down to the ground and return to mountain pose. Stand with awareness of standing, just as you began.

7. Repeat this sequence with the left foot.

8. When you are back in mountain pose again, mindfully pause. Bring awareness to your breath and let yourself be. Simply stand with awareness.

9. Conclude this practice by stretching out your body in a way that feels good to you. For instance, lift the arms overhead (or leave them at your sides) and extend through the length of your spine while you enjoy a deep breath. As you exhale, let the arms come back down to your sides.

10. Then return to mountain pose for standing meditation, balancing over your own two feet.

Compassion Meditation after a Natural Disaster

A lack of control is probably the most stressful experience we can have. When it comes to natural disasters, as well as pandemics, this lack of control is universal. There may be intense upheaval in our own lives, but we also become keenly aware of the suffering of others. They may even be hundreds of miles away, but our own hearts can be touched by others' fears and sorrows. There's a practice, quite ancient, called *tonglen*, or "taking and sending," where we hope to help alleviate others' suffering by taking it in and allowing it to touch our own heart, then breathing out comfort, healing, and goodness. This is a variation that was shared with me by a hospice nurse.

🕐 20 minutes

1. Take some time to settle inward and stabilize your attention with the breath or open monitoring. Sit with mindful awareness.

2. On an in breath, acknowledge your suffering or that of others.

3. On the out breath, offer compassion, hope, recognition, peace, or whatever you or the people you are holding may need. We don't have to know what that may be, so if you aren't sure, hold a space of loving-kindness.

4. Continue breathing this way. Inhale, acknowledging the suffering of others or yourself; exhale, offering compassion, hope, peace, or whatever you imagine would be helpful.

5. Every so often you may want to pause and simply rest in awareness. If there are tender emotions, recognize them. It is only natural for the heart to respond in this way. If there is a feeling of resistance or stoic resolve, that's okay, too. There's no right way to feel with this practice.

6. Finish by spending some time as you began with a focus on the breath or open monitoring.

Growing Older
with Grace

Through conscious aging, we can reap the benefits of our earned wisdom, applying it in a way that it adds to our resilience. Aging is not a one-time event, but rather a lifelong process. We can't see it happening from moment to moment, but it becomes evident over time. It may be how we look at ourselves in the mirror. It may be aches and pains that arise seemingly out of nowhere. It may be changes in our need for rest, or perhaps greater attention placed on self-care in a way we did not prioritize in our youth. A source of resilience as we age relates to sourcing the creativity and strengths that may have been dormant for quite some time as we attended to the responsibilities of our youth and middle years.

🕐 30 minutes (Use a timer.)

1. Take time for yourself. Consciously note that this is time just for you, away from responsibilities.

2. Stabilize your attention, either through focused breathing or just sitting with awareness.

3. Recognize any feelings present. If there are no specific feelings present, look for clues in bodily tension, restlessness, or ease.

4. Although feelings are temporary and constantly changing, they are also clues for our needs. When our needs are satisfied, they are more likely to be positive. When they are not satisfied, they are more likely to be negative. (Learn more about this in *Nonviolent Communication: A Language of Life*, by Marshall Rosenberg.)

5. Ask yourself, "What do I need today? What longing or creative act would bring me a sense of satisfaction?"

6. Whatever response arises, stay with it. Let it reverberate within you, as though you were a bell.

(continues)

7. Mindfully consider some action you may take today (or tomorrow, if you are meditating in the evening) that honors the need you have.

8. Until the timer goes off, continue using the breath to stabilize your attention. Sit with awareness, honoring the clarity of your wisdom and insight for taking care of you.

After a Traumatic Event

After any number of stressful events, there may be lingering fear, anxiety, self-blame, worry, and other symptoms. The dysregulation of the nervous system can be profound, and the mind may struggle to make sense of what happened. Recovery is a process that takes time. It can be supported, but not forced. Deep rest, if possible, can assist your body and mind in recuperating as the natural channels of healing work in the background. This meditation is based on a practice called "autogenic training," when our mind and body can support one another in getting deep rest.

🕐 30 minutes

Note: If you would like to change the wording, the phrases below may be adjusted to suit your preferences.

1. Find a quiet time and place to lie down where you can be uninterrupted.

2. Spend some time gently breathing in through the nose, and then, keeping the jaw relatively relaxed, exhaling through the mouth. Do this for a few cycles until you feel your body start to shift into a calmer state.

3. Breathing in, think "My arms and legs," breathing out, "are heavy and warm" (repeat six times).

4. Breathing in, think "My heartbeat is," breathing out, "slow and regular" (repeat six times).

5. Breathing in, think "My breathing is," breathing out, "free and flowing" (repeat six times).

6. Breathing in, think "My abdomen is," breathing out, "relaxed and calm" (repeat six times).

7. Breathing in, think "My mind is," breathing out, "serene and peaceful" (repeat six times).

(continues)

8. Breathing in think, "My body is," breathing out, "heavy and warm" (repeat six times).

9. You may finish by simply resting for as long as you'd like. Alternatively, picture yourself carrying this relaxed state into the rest of your day.

Reclaim Self-Trust after a Terminal Diagnosis

A terminal diagnosis will rock our worlds like a cataclysm. Many emotions, including times of feeling numb or wanting to withdraw, as well as strong emotions and a need for the support of others, can appear. This is a time to refine your relationship with yourself, to draw on an attitude of self-trust, no matter how things unfold. The attitudes of mindfulness (see page 10) can be a support. Draw on qualities like patience, self-kindness, and letting go of trying to create any specific experience. As you self-regulate the inner reactivity of body and mind, feel that you can trust this ability to find it, to arrive there. Self-trust highlights this capacity, which can always support you, including beyond the time of the meditation.

🕐 25 to 40 minutes (Use a timer.)

1. Take some time for yourself, at a time when you have the mental and emotional capacity to turn inward.

2. Connect with your experience of the breath. Think of the inhale and exhale like waves coming onto the shore. These waves can take any form, big or small, gentle or rough.

3. Continue breathing with mindful awareness as you head toward calmer waters, knowing that they are there even when conditions on the surface are turbulent or chaotic.

4. If thoughts or feelings become turbulent, stay with the waves of the breath. With time, you'll find the quieter waters.

5. Keep breathing and coming back to the breath each time the mind wanders or strong emotions arise.

6. Some days we reach the quieter waters more easily or quickly than others. Let go of trying to create any special kind of experience, and trust in the practice, that it can support you.

(continues)

7. As you meditate, trust that the meditation process will continue to develop, building mental and emotional resilience regardless of new conditions, however rough the surf. Stay with the waves of the breath.

8. Continue with the practice until the timer goes off.

PART III

Ongoing Practice

As we develop our mindfulness skills, they may be flexibly woven into the fabric of our lives. Consider that within changing conditions, there also tends to be a common thread that holds things together. This thread is a sense of connection to oneself. From this place, we have a vantage point that is both familiar and stable.

When we are in touch mindfully, we can respond to stressful situations in a way that lowers stress and improves communication, relationships, sleep quality, pain management, efficiency at work, immunity, and self-care. Mindfulness helps us feel happier. Let these next meditations offer additional opportunities to keep exploring how to weave mindfulness into your life in ways that are creative and personal.

Movement

While stress can lead to disconnection and imbalance, mindful movement restores these things. It can bring calm when we need it, but it can also lift our energy and our spirits when we feel depleted. Like a mini reset, mindful movement helps us realign our perspective on life, especially during times of stress. Stillness is not the only way to meditate!

Mindful movement goes beyond yoga to encompass a variety of embodied awareness practices. These can be calming, soothing, or gently energizing. They can help us calm down, relax, release tension, and feel refreshed any time of day. Moving meditations are also a great resource for when we would like to meditate but are feeling agitated or restless. The mindfulness we cultivate through movement practices easily carries over into other activities, because our bodies come with us wherever we go.

Neck and Shoulders Mindfulness Break

Here is a movement meditation that addresses the neck and shoulders, which are two regions of the body most prone to carrying tension when we are stressed. The benefits can linger for hours and are cumulative. Transitions between activities provide the perfect opportunity for mindfulness breaks like this. Examples include logging off your computer, getting in your car, first thing in the morning, standing at the microwave, or waiting for the shower water to heat. Being more comfortable in our bodies can improve the quality of our lives. Take a mindfulness break with this flowing sequence.

🕐 5 minutes or more (Timer optional.)

1. Stand or sit in a balanced way with your feet flat on the floor. If you're sitting, rather than lean back, move toward the front edge of the chair.

2. Elongate through the spine and lift through the top of your head. Think of rooting down through your tailbone. Feel the feet in contact with the floor.

3. With eyes open or closed, do some slow and mindful shoulder rolls. Take an entire breath to do a full rotation.

4. Keep going around, slowly, at least five times. Then change directions.

5. Pause for a moment and feel the sensations generated by the movement.

6. Now do some neck rolls. Breathe slowly and regularly while you gently roll your head around. You can think of drawing a large circle

in front of you with your nose. Take a whole breath to make your way around the full circle.

7. After a few times in one direction, go the other way. Do this at least five times, slowly.

8. When finished, pause and check in. If you notice benefits from the activity, remember them to inspire you for future practice.

Mindful Movement
Wake-Up Routine

Starting your day with mindful movement can set the stage for a day of greater ease and less stress. When you wake up and recognize that you are awake, remember your intention for some mindful movement. This can become part of your morning flow. Don't underestimate the benefits. If you do this regularly, your future self will look back and thank you.

Modifications: Instead of standing, you may do this sitting on the edge of the bed with your feet on the floor. Instead of lifting arms overhead, elongate through the spine and lift through the crown of your head, decompressing your spine, bringing a stretch into your torso, and creating some additional elevation.

🕐 5 minutes (Timer optional.)

1. The night before, as you're lying in bed, picture yourself waking up and getting out of bed effortlessly.

2. In the morning, as soon as you're awake, recall the intention and immediately get out of bed.

3. Standing by the bed, feel into what your body needs and do a full body stretch that feels just right.

4. Let go of judgments about being rested or unrested. Keep an open mind.

5. After the full body stretch, take a deep breath and let your shoulders drop down.

6. Take a very deep breath as you spread your arms wide, as though embracing the world. Exhale and wrap your arms around yourself, giving yourself a hug. Do this three to five times.

7. Extend your right arm overhead (or leave it at your side) and lean toward the left, creating a stretch in the side of your body. Afterward, do the other side.

8. Give yourself another hug (or leave your arms at your sides). Twist gently to the left, gazing over your left shoulder. Gently unwind back to the front and then go the other way.

9. Do another full body stretch. Shake out your hands. Mindfully check in: Ask yourself how you are feeling and if you have any special needs for your morning or your day.

A Bedtime Ritual

Bedtime, or the end of the day, can be a perfect time to relax physically, de-stress, and let the day have a soft finish. Yoga practice doesn't have to be a long and drawn-out activity. Sometimes the simpler, the better. You don't have to raise the bar for yourself, especially if you're feeling stressed; give yourself permission to do this with about 80 percent effort, especially if you tend to push yourself past your limits. This is a simple yoga sequence that you can integrate into your daily life.

🕐 3 to 5 minutes (Timer optional.)

1. Start by lying down, with your knees bent and feet flat on the floor or bed.

2. Bring your knees in toward your chest and give yourself a hug.

3. Take some mindful breaths. Recognize that the day is ending and no matter what kind of day you've had, this time is just for you.

4. Take some more mindful breaths and just let yourself be.

5. Hold the right knee into your chest and extend the left leg, giving it a gentle stretch. Pause a bit, and when you're ready, switch sides: Bring the left knee in toward the chest and extend the right leg out toward the opposite wall.

6. Invite your body to slow down further. Remind yourself that this is a time for unwinding and rest.

7. Bring both knees into the chest and once again, give yourself a hug.

8. Stretch your legs on the bed, floor, or wherever you are lying. Bring consciousness into your body and be heavy, like a bag of wet sand, to feel fully supported.

9. Spend some time breathing, slowly and regularly, just letting yourself be. Allow the day to officially come to a close. Tomorrow will be a fresh beginning.

Mindfulness at the Gym

Going to the gym can be infused with mindfulness so it becomes an informal kind of meditation. Mindfulness and fitness are a dynamic duo, and working out can be great stress relief and a change of scenery that refreshes the mind. It also is a social experience, and connection with others is good for our health. Maximize your workout experiences with the following guidance.

🕐 30 minutes or longer (Timer optional.)

1. Decide to make mindfulness a priority during a trip to the gym. Check in with your needs and decide on your goals.

2. As you enter the gym, recognize this transition and put outside responsibilities on pause to give yourself over fully to this experience. Think of mindfulness like a spotlight. Wherever attention goes, it clarifies and lights up what arises in awareness. No need to try to make it happen.

3. Mindfully note your visual experience. Look around mindfully; allow your eyes to be receptive to whatever comes into view. Let go of analyzing or judging for mindful seeing.

4. Next is hearing. Note the many sounds around you. Gyms can be loud. There's a virtual tapestry of sound. You don't have to do anything—except recognize mindful hearing.

5. When your mind gets distracted, invite attention back to being mindfully aware. Be mindful of where you are going and why.

6. As you begin a gym activity, recognize when you've become distracted. There's a lot here to notice. When you notice distractions, you are being mindful.

7. As you finish your last activity, ask yourself if there's anything you would like to remember for a future time. Recognize your accomplishment.

85. Moving Meditation at Work

Imagine for a moment your busiest day at work, the kind of day when you barely have time for yourself. Even days like this *can* include meditation. The secret is how to make work a kind of meditation practice. It can be helpful if there is a repetitive activity, and it's probably best not to do while you are online or immersed in email writing. However, any other mundane part of your day can work.

🕐 5 to 10 minutes (Timer optional.)

1. Recognize that you're stressed (perhaps feeling tense, breathing shallowly, or feeling nervous).

2. Whatever you're doing, regard your next routine activity as a time for informal meditation.

3. The key to this practice is being intentional and deliberate about mindfulness movement. Decide on the beginning of the activity or task and decide what will mark its completion.

4. Be mindfully present and aware. Notice how your body is oriented in the space where you are. Allow your eyes to be receptive to what is in view. Note shapes and colors, perhaps people. Become aware of sound. Simply recognize that they are occurring, near or far.

5. Bring awareness to a sense of your body and to sensations of movement. If possible, go a little more slowly than you usually do.

6. If other people are around, you don't have to shut them out. Recognize they're there. Perhaps give a simple acknowledgment like a head nod or smile. You can let it be clear, through body language, that you are focusing deliberately.

7. Keep bringing attention back to the breath or whatever is "home base" for your attention.

8. When you reach the conclusion of the activity you selected, take a moment's pause and a deep, intentional inhale and exhale.

Seasonal Sensory Awareness

Through sensory awareness, this meditation can help you stay connected to the cycles of seasons. It involves mindful movement, sensory awareness, and a chance to do meditation outdoors. If you plan to go outside, have shoes and possibly a jacket on or close by before you begin.

🕐 10 minutes (Timer optional.)

1. Take an intentional sitting posture indoors. As you sit, breathing mindfully, reflect on the current season. Recall anything you have noticed that reflects the present time of year.

2. Mindfully stand and go outside or go to a window and look out. Open to your senses. Mindfully listen: Are sounds clear or muffled? Is there wind? What are you seeing? What color is the sky? Are there clouds? If so, what kind? Is the sun shining? If it's nighttime, can you see the moon or stars?

3. Look about and find a twig, flower, or leaf. Notice why it gets your attention. In what way does it reflect the current season? Is there a sense of pleasure or other feelings? Memories? If you can, touch it, hold it in your hand (or just in your mind).

4. Bring the object back indoors with you, if you can, and place it somewhere that you can see it to remind you of this time of year. Alternatively, identify something in your place that can remind you. It may even be just a note to yourself.

5. Pause, close your eyes, and just let yourself be. What would you like to remember from this experience?

Mindful Running, Swimming, and Cycling

With practice, many forms of exercise can become a chance to meditate. It can be great stress relief to exercise and let your mind go, or to become immersed in the activity. But mindfulness is about consciousness. When we are very active, there are even more things that will grab our attention. This is the challenge of meditating while being very active. Draw upon the attitudes of mindfulness like patience, non-striving, self-trust, curiosity, beginner's mind, and acceptance for support. They can help your exercise practice become a meditation, both intentional and aware. Your attitude and mindful awareness of mind, body, and your surroundings can support you with this practice.

🕐 10 to 30 minutes (Timer optional.)

1. Choose a routine exercise or sports activity that you like to do. Consciously decide how much time will specifically be a dedicated meditation practice.

2. Pause before beginning. Take a moment to be quiet and check in with yourself. Note your state of mind, how your body is feeling, and any emotions present or the mood you're in.

3. Resolve to recognize when your mind has wandered, and then bring it back to your breath. The breath and body sensations will be your primary anchors for attention.

4. Slowly begin the activity and remain aware of sensations, of breathing, and of your body moving.

5. When you recognize you've become lost in thought or distracted away from the breath and body, bring attention back.

6. If you become entangled in thoughts or distractions, there is the choice of dropping the thought and coming back to body and mind, or you can take a little time to note it and how you would like to take action on it later. Then resume awareness of breath and body.

7. When the meditation concludes, check in. Would you like to remember anything for a future time?

Focused Senses, New Perspective

This meditation can help you wake up your senses to the novelty available even in a place you know well. Each new moment is a new beginning and a fresh start. The informal meditation here is to be mindful of the way even small changes can introduce new perspective and refresh our mindset. When we're stressed, familiarity may be a comfort, but sometimes a change of perspective is good medicine.

🕐 5 to 10 minutes

1. Put other activities and responsibilities on pause as you take some mindful breaths to center yourself.

2. Mentally reflect: What would it be like if you were brand-new to the place you live, your neighborhood, your job, where you shop, and the things you buy?

3. Decide on something to do differently, for a half day, a day, or a week.

    - Mindfully shop at a different grocery store.
    - Drive on different streets to get to work or other familiar places.
    - Eat at a restaurant you've never been to, or order something entirely new.

4. Later, when you do your chosen activity, notice how you feel, emotionally and physically, engaging with something routine that also involves the unfamiliar. How does it affect your mood or mental state?

5. Each day, check in and note how these mindful changes may be introducing a new perspective. If you'd like, spend some time mindfully journaling about what you have learned about yourself or where you live.

Mindful Energy

Whether starting off your day or giving yourself a gentle boost, integrating this sequence of movements can bring balance and fresh energy into your life. This is an activity called "meridian tapping." It comes from the system of mindful movement called qigong. You'll do this with the palm of your hand by tapping, patting, or cupping the skin of your torso, arms, and legs. Tap hard enough that you can feel some sensations in the skin, like vibrating, tingling, heat, or whatever you notice. You can take an entire minute or longer with each region.

🕐 20 minutes (timer recommended but optional)

1. Take an upright posture and invite some focus through mindful breathing.

2. **Left arm:** Using the palm of your right hand, begin tapping or patting the back of the left hand, moving up the outside of the left arm all the way to the shoulder. Tap or pat yourself gently on your back, and then move to the front, tapping along your collarbone to the center of your chest, then back out to the shoulder and down the inside of your left arm to the palm.

3. **Right arm:** Do the same sequence on the right.

4. **Torso:** Move the hands to the abdomen area and use a cupping motion. Pat the front of your abdomen and lower torso. Do it hard enough to feel sensations like vibrations under your hands. Then move around to the lower back and pat in the region of the lower back.

5. **Legs:** Tap or pat down the backs of the legs to the feet, and then up the front of the legs.

6. **Eyes:** Rub your palms together vigorously, generating warmth, and cup them gently over your eyes. Let your eyes relax and take in that warmth.

(continues)

7. **Head:** Using your fingertips, gently tap all over your scalp, moving around all over the head.

8. **Sweeping:** Go over all the areas you were tapping, but instead of tapping, use a sweeping motion, as if you were covered in dust and were trying to brush it off.

9. **To complete:** Stand upright. Take the hands and rest them over your lower abdomen, one on top of the other. Pause and breathe mindfully.

Note: If standing isn't right for your body, do this sitting in a chair. The back-tapping portion can be accommodated by leaning forward.

Sundown Meditation

The daily cycle of light and dark forms the backdrop of our lives. When we're busy or stressed, we may miss out on these magical transitions. This standing meditation (which may also be done sitting) involves watching the sun go down. It is especially nice to do at times of the year when days are short and night comes early, like at the winter solstice. Before your eyes, your experience of the landscape is transformed. Witnessing these transitions while meditating with eyes open may remain in your memory for a long time to come.

🕐 30 minutes (Timer optional.)

1. About 20 minutes before dark, stand or sit by a window where you can see outside. (Alternatively, do this outdoors.) Keep your eyes open (it's fine to keep blinking naturally, however).

2. Adopt an intentional standing or sitting meditation posture. Feel your feet in contact with the floor. Let your arms and hands relax at your sides or lap. Breathe with awareness.

3. Mindfully gaze outdoors at the sky and whatever else comes into view. Let your eyes take in everything that appears before you. This could be the color of the sky, the shapes of clouds, the trees, houses, buildings, birds, animals, people—anything at all. Be particularly aware of the quality of light. Bring your mind back when it wanders.

4. As you see mindfully, watch how the light gradually changes. Colors start to fade, and the edges of things may become less distinct. If there are still light sources about, watch how they illuminate the surrounding space.

5. Finish with a few mindful breaths, noting how you feel after taking part in this transition of day to night. As you move into the rest of your evening, try to stay in touch with what you felt while experiencing the transition.

Five-Minute Meditations

One might think that if a little meditation is good, longer must be better. In actuality, it is regular practice done consistently that yields the best long-term results. An attitude of "more is better" has deflated many a meditation practice. Five minutes is a generally accessible amount of time and more than enough. I have noticed that the world can look very different to me after just a five-minute practice. Give yourself the gift of five minutes on a busy day.

When it feels like meditation won't fit in your life because it takes too much time, think again. Everyone can reclaim a few minutes here or there. Making yourself a priority can take a little practice, but it reaps big rewards. Small islands of mindfulness meditation can help you recharge with a big return on your investment.

Morning Peace

Days often flow so much more smoothly when we meditate early on. Even if our minds are filled with thoughts about to-do items, tasks, and responsibilities, there is something about "the light of awareness" that helps with internal organization. When the mind is "thinking," it truly is doing its job, even when we'd prefer some quiet. In this meditation, we'll acknowledge thoughts with a "thank-you," while creating the right conditions for the mind to gradually recognize it can take a break. You don't have to feel the benefits during the time of practice. They happen in the background, often on a level we can't consciously detect.

🕐 5 minutes (Use a timer.)

1. Go to your meditation spot (chosen in advance). As you sit down and settle in, let your body become heavy, like a bag of potting soil or sack of flour. Feel the full support of where you're sitting.

2. Bring attention to the feeling of your breath flowing in and out. See if you can gather all your attention and bring it to focus on the breath—one breath at a time.

3. When the mind wanders, recognize what's on your mind and note it with a thank-you.

4. Acknowledge the thought, and come back to the breath.

5. Repeat steps 3 and 4 until your timer goes off.

6. When the timer sounds, take a moment to thank yourself for giving you this time. Before you begin again tomorrow, reflect on how meditating may have positively impacted your day.

Late-Night Tranquility

Often when we're awake late at night, it's because our body and mind are still revved up from the day. We might prefer to hurry up and get sleepy, but we can't force this to happen. What we can do is create the right conditions for the mind to become more peaceful and all the alert signals that tell you to stay mentally active can calm down. The focus, in part, is learning how to recognize when you're "sleepy-tired" so that when you get in bed, you can just drift off to sleep. Here's how to practice.

🕐 5 minutes (Timer optional; you might want to just drift off to sleep.)

1. Go to a spot where you can sit or lie down, preferably a place other than your bed. This can be anywhere you can relax until you get sleepy-tired.

2. Recognize how you're feeling in body and mind. Whether tense, exhausted, irritated, afraid, worried, agitated, or just wide awake, acknowledge it.

3. Take a deep breath, pause at the top of the inhale for 5 to 10 seconds, then slowly release the breath. Repeat twice for a total of three times.

4. Feel the sensations of breathing, specifically in your chest. Notice that when you breathe in, the breathing muscles and skin contract, and as you breathe out, they relax. Continue noticing the contracting and relaxing of these areas.

5. Either continue with the relaxed breathing, or with an inner voice that is as calm and reassuring as you can imagine, speak to yourself inwardly, saying, "Relax [your name]" slowly and caringly for the entire exhale.

6. When the timer goes off (if you used one), decide if you are sleepy-tired yet, and if not, you may consider repeating the meditation as many times as desired.

In-a-Pinch
Anxiety Reduction

Over the course of our lives, we'll likely encounter circumstances when we have less control than we might like. For example, most of us would prefer not to experience heavy turbulence on an airplane, medical tests, trips to the dentist, or being in court. Amid any stressful situation or place, there's a haven of support that you might not recognize if you aren't being mindful. Here's how you can use awareness to find support and peace, even during a stressful time or event.

🕐 5 minutes (Timer optional.)

1. Choose to pay attention. Look around and allow what you're seeing to register. Let your eyes relax and be receptive to what comes into view.

2. Recognize shapes and colors, people, objects, the room where you are, and anything else that comes to your attention. Let go of labels or figuring things out, and just mindfully see without judging or analyzing.

3. Note any feelings, judgments, preferences, or emotional reactions. As you look around, you'll probably find that some of what you notice is pleasant, some of it neutral (you neither particularly like or don't like it), and some of it even unpleasant.

4. The distinctions might be subtle, but keep bringing your attention back to whatever is pleasant or neutral. You may even notice that your body or mind will relax a little bit when you do so. You can choose where to put your attention.

5. While maintaining this attention to neutral, breathe slowly and regularly. Use the breath to help your body self-regulate around anxiety and stress.

6. Continue to practice for about five minutes. If you wish to go longer, the practice is here for you.

Book Collection Meditation

When we see the big picture, it can place worries in perspective and remind us of our strengths, talents, and what holds meaning for us. Many of us, over the years, have developed a collection of books. Whether read or unread, along with the stories contained therein, they also can tell a story about your own life. They may have a message of support for you, even if you don't read a word more. Go to your books for this meditation on meaning and perspective.

🕐 5 minutes (Use a timer.)

1. Go wherever you keep your books. Before doing anything else, pause and check in. How are you feeling? Is there anything on your mind or weighing on your heart?

2. With receptive eyes, take in the books. Without judgment, just scan across them and see what's here. Recognize the covers, the shapes, the colors.

3. When ready, pick up one of the books. Any book. Just let yourself be drawn to it, without giving it too much thought.

4. Hold the book you have chosen and check in again. Are there thoughts coming to mind? Feelings or memories? Ideas or plans? You might consider thanking the book, and then put it back.

5. Go through the same process again. Recognize that some books get your attention more than others. Remember or identify why you are holding on to each book you touch.

6. When the timer sounds, put the last book you're holding back on the shelf.

7. Check in and ask yourself if there's a book here that has something to offer you at this time in your life, or perhaps something you would like to release to lighten your load.

Journey to Tranquility

During stressful times in the past, have you ever wished you were somewhere else? The mind is a powerful instrument. It's possible to use our imagination in a way that brings us to a place of calm. It's available anytime you remember that it's there for you. Give it a try right now or sometime you'd like to take your mind off worries. You can also use this meditation to help you fall asleep.

🕐 5 minutes (Use a timer.)

1. Sit or lie down in a way that you can be comfortable for a while. Close your eyes and do three cycles of long, slow breathing. Make the breath of even duration on the in and out.

2. Recall or imagine a location where you felt or could imagine feeling relaxed, content, happy, peaceful, or any other quality that would feel good to you right now.

3. As you think of this place, fill in as many details as you can. Is it indoors or outdoors? Is it in nature, a city, or somewhere else? What do you like about it? In your mind recognize what evokes the positive feelings. Is it the actual location, the meaning it holds, or something else?

4. Picture yourself walking or moving about in this place, and imagine it detail by detail, every step, every feeling. What do you imagine your body would feel like? Are you picturing yourself alone or with others?

5. Is there anything from your mind journey you would like to bring into the rest of your day or evening?

Daily Practice for Cultivating Happiness

We can take actions that are likely to help us feel happier. The following meditation is a reflection you can do every day, as well as put into action. Give it a try daily for a week, and afterward reflect on how any aspect of the practice has influenced your everyday life: body, mind, sense of connection to others, sense of well-being, pain, sleep, creativity, driving, and so on.

🕐 5 minutes (Use a timer.)

1. At the end of the day or a time of your choosing, take some time to center yourself in a relaxed way. You can sit or lie down, be indoors or outdoors—it doesn't matter where. For the sake of regularity, you might consider making this a ritual, and do it in the same place and at the same time every day.

2. Close your eyes and picture the kind of day you have had, or reflect on the last 24 hours.

3. How are you feeling now, in body, mind, and spirit?

4. Take some centering breaths and invite yourself to relax. Put on hold unfinished tasks, things yet to be started, or anything else. This is time just for you.

5. When ready, reflect on the following three things:

   - Recall something good that happened to you within the last 24 hours.
   - Recall a good deed you did (even better if you're the only one who knows about it).
   - What are three things you are grateful for?

6. If you finish with these contemplations before the timer goes off, spend extra time savoring the satisfaction, gratitude, happiness, ease, or whatever else arose from the experiences you noted, however big or small.

Stress Relief
through Music

Our mind tends to respond to what we point it toward. All it takes is a few minutes to get your bearings and incline your mind in a less-stressed direction. Recognizing this could change your life. We can start to prefer calm to drama—and recognize when we make related choices. For this meditation, we're going to use some calming music. Find a piece of music you find calming. (One of mine is "The Lark Ascending" by Vaughan Williams.) Music without words is helpful, because lyrics may cause the mind to become more active rather than to settle.

🕐 5 minutes, more or less—whatever the length of the music you've chosen

1. Find a comfortable posture and settle in for some stillness. Whatever you are feeling, whether stressed, anxious, physically uncomfortable, or anything else, recognize that this is a time just for you. Even amid these challenges, however unpleasant, you can incline the mind toward the goodness that is also here.

2. Put on the music, if you haven't already, and settle in to mindfully listen. Immerse yourself in the details of the music. Get curious. When the mind wanders, bring it back to appreciating the music.

3. Let attention rest on the musical notes, just as at other times it might rest on the breath or something else. Give all your attention to listening mindfully.

4. When the music ends, you may want to stay longer, but five minutes is enough for reclaiming perspective. It's here for you whenever you need it.

Envisioning the
Future You Want

Our mind has great influence over our life, through our thoughts, moods, attitudes, impulses, and more. Much of this is unconscious. You can use mindfulness to embrace the powers of the mind, to consciously steer it toward a happier future or whatever it is you want. This meditation will use a visualization practice. It could be used for envisioning the distant future, but let's start with a better tomorrow.

🕐 5 minutes (Use a timer.)

1. Take some time for yourself to meditate. As you settle, recognize your mood, feelings, state of mind, or present attitude.

2. Breathe mindfully. You may recognize that sometimes it feels more satisfying to take deeper breaths, or that you like breathing quietly right now. Choose to breathe in a way that feels good to you.

3. What is on your plate for tomorrow? It may or may not take place in the way you think it will, but how would you like your day tomorrow to unfold? What would make tomorrow a really great day?

4. Walk through it in your mind. Starting with waking up, mentally envision your day with as much detail as possible.

5. Make it realistic. For example, visualize yourself struggling with a project (if you are), but then having a breakthrough and being happy about it. How would you look when feeling happy like that? How would you feel in your body?

6. Go through the day to its conclusion, and then picture yourself being satisfied and content. If you expect a hard day, picture yourself relieved.

7. When the timer goes off, take a moment to note anything you would like to remember from this activity. You might even want to jot down some notes for future reference.

The Power of Just Sitting

The mind can have support while also being given freedom. This practice, which is alternatively referred to as just sitting, open awareness, or choiceless awareness, involves simply resting in awareness. Whatever arises in the mind or gets your attention is constantly changing. Enjoy the flexibility of this spacious practice, and simply let yourself be with what's happening. The future will take care of itself. Notice the freedom of choice and how there is nothing required of you.

🕐 5 minutes (Use a timer.)

1. Put tasks and responsibilities on pause so you can claim this time for yourself. Find a posture that feels supportive, and just let yourself be.

2. There's no need to focus on anything. Not the breath, not body, not sound. No need to give attention to thoughts or even feelings. Just let yourself be, taking a break from all doing, fixing, planning, remembering—everything.

3. You can either track or let go of tracking. Make this easy on yourself: If it helps to have an anchor, like the breath or body sensations, draw on it. But if it feels easier to let go of tracking anything, you can choose to do nothing.

4. Keep going until you hear the timer sound. Check in and notice how you are feeling. If this spacious practice resonates with you, know that it is here for you anytime or anyplace you need it.

Midday Refresher

The middle of the day appears to be like no-man's land when it comes to meditation. Many say that first thing in the morning or the end of the day is when their days are more predictable. During the day, plans can change, and we also may be affected by things over which we have little or no control. What might it feel like to take some control back? Give this meditation a try to learn how. Let this help you decide what to do for yourself.

🕐 5 minutes (Use a timer.)

1. When you find that you're able to take a little time for yourself, check in and ask yourself what is most needed right now. First cover your basic needs:

    - Are you hungry?
    - Tired?
    - Feeling certain emotions?
    - How does your body feel?

2. Let go of assumptions and check in further. Identify a way you might refresh your senses in some way.

    - A change of place?
    - Invigorating your sense of smell?
    - Sense of hearing or listening (music, birds, running water, silence, etc.)?
    - Sense of taste?
    - Visuals (colors, textures, shapes, nature, artwork, etc.)?

3. Do you need something?

    - Social time?
    - Alone time?
    - Creativity?
    - Doing-nothing time?

(continues)

4. Picture yourself taking action to meet the needs you have identified. If it doesn't feel right when you try it on for size in your mind, recognize that and choose something else. What you settle on might surprise you.

5. When the timer goes off, take this deeper understanding and try doing something for yourself that can take care of your needs in some way, even if it is small. You'll be sending a clear message of self-care to your body and mind, and making strides to build your resilience.

BEGINNINGS
AND ENDINGS

Meditation is not a transformation where you suddenly feel calm or have a mind free of thoughts. It's often when we look back from a new phase of life that we can see how our meditation practice changed our trajectory—our stress went down, or we reclaimed a life otherwise lost to distractions and habitual patterns.

Each day, our meditation sessions may end, but the meditation path is one that keeps going. Consider each conscious breath as a fresh start, an opportunity to begin again. Keep going. There are many who walk this path along with you. Check out the Resources section on the next page for additional ways to keep learning and growing. I honor you on your continued journey.

RESOURCES

Recommended Books

Bays, Jan Chozen. *Mindful Eating: A Guide to Rediscovering a Healthy and Joyful Relationship with Food*, rev. ed. Boulder, CO: Shambhala, 2017.

Brahm, Ajahn. *Kindfulness*. Boston: Wisdom Publications, 2016.

Fogg, B. J. *Tiny Habits: The Small Changes That Change Everything.* Boston: Houghton Mifflin Harcourt, 2019.

Goldstein, Joseph. *The Path of Insight Meditation*. Boulder, CO: Shambhala, 2018.

Gunaratana, Bhante Henepola. *Mindfulness in Plain English*. Boston: Wisdom Publications, 2011.

Hanson, Rick. *Buddha's Brain: The Practical Neuroscience of Happiness, Love, and Wisdom*. Oakland, CA: New Harbinger, 2009.

Kabat-Zinn, Jon. *Full Catastrophe Living: Using the Wisdom of Your Body and Mind to Face Stress, Pain, and Illness*, rev. ed. New York: Bantam, 2013.

Kabat-Zinn, Jon. *Mindfulness for Beginners: Reclaiming the Present Moment—and Your Life*. Boulder, CO: Sounds True, 2012.

Kabat-Zinn, Jon. *Wherever You Go, There You Are: Mindfulness Meditation in Everyday Life*. New York: Hyperion, 2005.

Kornfield, Jack. *A Path with Heart: A Guide through the Perils and Promises of Spiritual Life*. New York: Bantam Books, 1993.

Neff, Kristin. *Self-Compassion: The Proven Power of Being Kind to Yourself*. New York: Harper Collins, 2015.

Nhat Hanh, Thich. *The Miracle of Mindfulness: An Introduction to the Practice of Meditation*, rev. ed. Boston: Beacon Press, 2016.

Nhat Hanh, Thich. *Peace Is Every Breath: A Practice for Our Busy Lives*. New York: HarperOne, 2011.

Rosenberg, Marshall. *Nonviolent Communication: A Language of Life*. Encinitas, CA: PuddleDancer Press, 2005.

Salzberg, Sharon. *Loving-kindness: The Revolutionary Art of Happiness*. Boston: Shambhala, 1995.

Sofer, Oren Jay. *Say What You Mean: A Mindful Approach to Nonviolent Communication*. Boulder, CO: Shambhala, 2018.

Suzuki, Shunryu. *Zen Mind, Beginner's Mind*, 50th anniversary ed. Edited by Trudy Dixon. Boulder, CO: Shambhala, 2020.

Young, Shinzen. *Natural Pain Relief: How to Sooth and Dissolve Physical Pain with Mindfulness*. Boulder, CO: Sounds True, 2011.

Apps

Calm (calm.com)

Headspace (headspace.com)

Insight Timer (insighttimer.com)

MyLife (my.life)

Websites

Boroson, Martin. "One-Moment Meditation: How to Meditate in a Moment." YouTube.com, March 2, 2011. youtu.be/F6eFFCi12v8.

Mindfulness-Based Stress Reduction Programs (MBSR). "Guided Meditations." Led by Denise Dempsey, MEd, and others. stressreductionprograms.com/meditations.

Mindfulness Training

The Center for Nonviolent Communication provides training and other services aiming to foster compassionate and "life-serving" human relations in a broad range of areas, including personal change, relationships, at work, and healthcare. Available globally (cnvc.org).

East Coast Mindfulness provides premier online teaching and training in mindfulness, plus MBSR live online programs, and has a listing of MBSR teachers certified to teach MBSR live online (eastcoastmindfulness.com).

Eight-Week Mindful Self-Compassion class sessions include a variety of meditative practice and exercises in which participants explore the experience of self-compassion, examine common obstacles to self-compassion, and learn techniques for cultivating self-compassion in daily life. A course directory can be found on the website for the Center for Mindful Self-Compassion (centerformsc.org).

Eight-Week Mindfulness-Based Stress Reduction (MBSR) Program, the time-tested and evidence-based eight-week immersion in mindfulness, is relatively low cost and has proven high-yield benefits. An internet search for a certified MBSR instructor will reveal high-quality eight-week programs in your area and online worldwide.

Wisdom 2.0 hosts annual conferences and online events that focus on living with mindfulness, wisdom, and compassion. The annual conference is attended by both those interested in mindfulness and global leaders, speakers, and mindfulness teachers (wisdom2conference.com).

Retreat Centers

Insight Meditation Society, Barre, MA (dharma.org)

Shambhala Mountain Center, Red Feather Lakes, CO
(shambhalamountain.org)

Spirit Rock Meditation Center, Woodacre, CA (spiritrock.org)

REFERENCES

Black, David S., Gillian A. O'Reilly, Richard Olmstead, Elizabeth C. Breen, and Michael R. Irwin. "Mindfulness Meditation and Improvement in Sleep Quality and Daytime Impairment among Older Adults with Sleep Disturbances." *JAMA Internal Medicine* 175, no. 4 (January 2015): 494–501. https://www.ncbi.nlm.nih.gov/pmc/articles/PMC4407465.

Cuddy, Amy J. C., S. Jack Schultz, and Nathan E. Fosse. "*P*-Curving a More Comprehensive Body of Research on Postural Feedback Reveals Clear Evidential Value for Power-Posing Effects: Reply to Simmons and Simonsohn (2017)." *Psychological Science* 29, no. 4 (February 2018): 656–66. https://journals.sagepub.com/eprint/CzbNAn7Ch6ZZirK9yMGH/full.

Dixon, M. L., C. Moodie, P. Goldin, N. Farb, R. Heimberg, and J. J. Gross. "Emotion Regulation in Social Anxiety Disorder: Reappraisal and Acceptance of Negative Self-beliefs." *Biological Psychiatry: Cognitive Neuroscience and Neuroimaging* 5, no. 1 (January 2020): 119–29. https://www.biologicalpsychiatrycnni.org/article/S2451-9022(19)30202-2/fulltext.

Gasnier, M., A. Pelissolo, G. Bondolfi, S. Pelissolo, M. Tomba, L. Mallet, and K. N'diaye. "Mindfulness-Based Interventions in Obsessive-Compulsive Disorder: Mechanisms of Action and Presentation of a Pilot Study." *L'encephale* 43, no. 4 (December 2017): 594–99. https://europepmc.org/article/med/27887679.

Goldin, P., and J. Gross. "Effects of Mindfulness-Based Stress Reduction (MBSR) on Emotion Regulation in Social Anxiety Disorder." *Emotion* 10, no. 1 (February 2010): 83–91. https://www.ncbi.nlm.nih.gov/pubmed/20141305.

Goldin P., K. McRae, W. Ramel, Gross J. "The Neural Basis of Emotion Regulation: Reappraisal and Suppression of Negative Emotion." *Biological Psychiatry* 63, no. 6 (March 2008): 577–86. https://www .ncbi.nlm.nih.gov/pubmed/17888411.

Jha, A. P., A. B. Morrison, S. C. Parker, and E. A. Stanley. "Practice Is Protective: Mindfulness Training Promotes Cognitive Resilience in High-Stress Cohorts." *Mindfulness* 8 (January 2016): 46–58. https:// umindfulness.as.miami.edu/_assets/pdf/mindfulness-2016.pdf.

Kajimura, Shogo, Naoki Masuda, Johnny King Lau, and Kou Murayama. "Focused Attention Meditation Changes the Boundary and Configuration of Functional Networks in the Brain" (preprint). bioRxiv 664573 (July 2019). https://www.biorxiv.org/content /10.1101/664573v2.article-info.

Killingsworth, Matt. "Does Mind-Wandering Make You Unhappy?" *Greater Good Magazine* (July 16, 2013). https://greatergood.berkeley .edu/article/item/does_mind_wandering_make_you_unhappy.

Kurth, Florian, Nicolas Cherbuin, and Eileen Luders. "Promising Links between Meditation and Reduced (Brain) Aging: An Attempt to Bridge Some Gaps between the Alleged Fountain of Youth and the Youth of the Field." *Frontiers in Psychology* 8 (2017): 860. https://www.ncbi.nlm .nih.gov/pmc/articles/PMC5447722.

Lazar, S. W., C. E. Kerr, R. H. Wasserman, J. R. Gray, D. N. Greve, M. T. Treadway, M. McGarvey, et al. "Meditation Experience Is Associated with Increased Cortical Thickness." *NeuroReport* 16, no. 17 (November 2005): 1893–97. https://www.ncbi.nlm.nih.gov/pubmed/16272874.

Leary, Mark R., Eleanor B. Tate, Claire E. Adams, Ashley Batts Allen, and Jessica Hancock. "Self-Compassion and Reactions to Unpleasant Self-Relevant Events: The Implications of Treating Oneself Kindly." *Journal of Personality and Social Psychology* 92, no. 5 (2007): 887–904. https://self-compassion.org/wp-content/uploads/publications /LearyJPSP.pdf.

Shangraw, R., and V. L. Akhtar. (2016). "Mindfulness and Exercise." In *Current Perspectives in Social and Behavioral Sciences: Mindfulness and Performance*, edited by A. L. Baltzell, 300–20. Cambridge, UK: Cambridge University Press, 2016. https://psycnet.apa.org/record /2016-06592-012.

Wielgosz, Joseph, Simon B. Goldberg, Tammi R. A. Kral, John D. Dunne, and Richard J. Davidson. "Mindfulness Meditation and Psychopathology." *Annual Review of Clinical Psychology* 15, no. 1 (2019): 285–316. https://www.annualreviews.org/doi/abs/10.1146 /annurev-clinpsy-021815-093423.

ACKNOWLEDGMENTS

Writing this book has been an opportunity both to draw on my expertise as an MBSR teacher and also to learn and grow while doing so. The expertise has come through teaching and many hours of meditation practice and residential retreats, but also from the inspiration, guidance, and support of some key people. While writing during the time of COVID-19, I found the following to be particularly notable: Benjamin Nelson, Dylan Wright, Philippe Goldin, Rob Woodman, Soma Aloia, Yuriko Howell, and the weekly MBSR Student Alumni group. I have been inspired by my first meditation teacher, my now 95-year-old father, Al Groncki. I could not have done this without longtime friends and fellow teachers Beth Mulligan and David Spound, who have been stalwart and dedicated MBSR explorers with me since my earliest days as a teacher. Last but not least, I thank my editor, Erin Nelson, who helped polish this book into the gem I believe it has become.

ABOUT THE AUTHOR

 **Denise G. Dempsey, MEd,** enjoys combining her love of teaching with her lifelong interest in meditation and holistic health. Since 2003 Denise has dedicated her career to offering Mindfulness-Based Stress Reduction programs, both in person and now online. Denise holds a master of education degree in curriculum and instruction from Concordia University, in Portland, Oregon, and a bachelor of science in human development from UC Davis. She was certified to teach Mindfulness-Based Stress Reduction by the Center for Mindfulness at UMASS Medical School. She is also a certified MBSR Live Online teacher and a Tiny Habits® coach. Visit her website, StressReductionPrograms.com.